Contents

Executive summary	3
Introduction and overview	5
Part I: CGE Models of Trade Liberalisation in Practice	8
Micro-economic foundations	8
Operational model details	13
Model specification and macro causality in a closed economy	14
Open economy (Armington) macro-economics	17
The Armington fiscal effect	22
Part II: Simulations and Results	25
Aim and scope	25
Comparing models – our model versus World Bank models	25
Results	32
Conclusions	41
References	43
Appendix 1: The Social Accounting Matrix (SAM)	45
Appendix 2: The Model in Algebra	49
Acknowledgements	57
Endnotes	58

© Oxfam International 2007

This is a print version of a report originally issued online as *Modelling the Impact of Trade Liberalisation* at
www.oxfam.org.uk/what_we_do/issues/trade/research_trade_liberalisation.htm

The online report was uploaded in July 2006.
This print version, first published January 2007, is the authoritative edition.

ISBN 978 0 85598 585 1

This publication is copyright, but may be used free of charge for the purposes of advocacy, campaigning, education, and research, provided that the source is acknowledged in full. The copyright holder requests that all such use be registered with them for impact assessment purposes. For copying in any other circumstances, or for re-use in other publications, or for translation or adaptation, permission must be secured and a fee may be charged. For permission or further information, please e-mail publish@oxfam.org.uk.

Oxfam International is a confederation of thirteen organisations working together in more than 100 countries to find lasting solutions to poverty and injustice: Oxfam America, Oxfam Australia, Oxfam-in-Belgium, Oxfam Canada, Oxfam France – Agir Ici, Oxfam Germany, Oxfam Great Britain, Oxfam Hong Kong, Intermón Oxfam (Spain), Oxfam Ireland, Oxfam New Zealand, Oxfam Novib (Netherlands), and Oxfam Québec. Please call or write to any of the agencies for further information, or visit www.oxfam.org.

Disclaimer

This Oxfam Research Report was written to inform policy development on trade issues and as a background paper for the Oxfam Poverty Report (forthcoming in 2008).
It is published in order to share widely the results of Oxfam-commissioned research.
The views expressed in the report are those of the authors and do not necessarily reflect Oxfam's views.
For further information on the issues raised in this paper, please e-mail enquiries@oxfam.org.uk or go to www.oxfam.org

Executive summary

Trade models are of tremendous political importance. By pretending to see into the future and putting numbers on the 'welfare gains' accruing from trade liberalisation, such models have provided irresistible ammunition to negotiators, particularly those advocating rapid opening. At the Hong Kong WTO ministerial in December 2005, the press conferences of major players such as Robert Portman (USA) and Peter Mandelson (EU) were sprinkled with the findings of trade models, presented as fact. The incessant repetition of benefit numbers in many billions of dollars inevitably puts those advocating a more cautious approach to liberalisation on the defensive, even when such caution is fully warranted (not only by the mixed experience in recent decades of trade liberalisation in practice, but also by the weaknesses of 'typical' CGE models, as this paper clearly demonstrates).

The paper presents a review and critique of the most widely used trade models based on computable general equilibrium (or CGE) models. The emphasis throughout is on methodology. The paper provides concise analytical arguments explaining the fundamental weaknesses of CGE models, paying particular attention to the way that CGE models conceptualise and measure welfare. The authors also show that the manner in which the World Bank uses CGE modelling is highly problematic, making implausible assumptions about elasticities, the exchange rate, and macro causality. World Bank models assume that the most central macro-economic indicators do not change in response to any liberalisation scenario. The authors argue that this is negligent, especially in developing countries with historically large trade deficits, significant debt problems, and a large informal economy with underemployment in modern sectors. The authors also identify a particular inconsistency inherent in the use of 'Armington' specifications of elasticities in CGE models. They show that, even if the Bank's welfare measures and macro causal scheme are accepted, the welfare gains that liberalisation is supposed to induce are estimated incorrectly in LINKAGE, GTAP, and other trade models that adopt the popular Armington specification of imperfect competition between trading partners.

Using a table-top two-region and three-sector CGE model which represents sub-Saharan Africa and the rest of the world, the authors illustrate that the results of modelling are radically different when alternative, and more plausible, assumptions are made. Although the authors' model still incorporates a great deal of LINKAGE's lack of realism, it provides unambiguous policy insights:

- If trade elasticities are lower than the World Bank stipulates, sub-Saharan Africa faces welfare losses even in an otherwise optimistic situation which rules out all macro-economic shocks.

- If the current account is allowed to respond to trade liberalisation, and imports to one region grow stronger than that region's exports, it is Africa – and not the developed world – that faces a deteriorating trade balance.

- If the analysis includes government deficits, the African public balance often deteriorates, whereas the rest of the world's fiscal position improves.

- If employment and income are variable, they might very well increase in sub-Saharan Africa, but do so in tandem with mounting trade deficits and foreign debt, which renders these advances temporary.

The paper concludes that developing countries would be ill-advised to follow the radical recommendations of the World Bank's liberalisation strategy insofar as it rests on results drawn from the current trade models. The paper appeals for 'honest' simulation strategies showing the variety of outcomes that result from a range of plausible assumptions. These would enable policy makers to assess the different scenarios for themselves.

CGE models can be useful quantitative supplements to experimental thinking about the importance of different potential causal linkages among economic variables at the country or world level. However, mechanically churning out 'projections' of welfare gains or any other indicator subject to one single set of causal assumptions and parameter values is a fundamental misuse of a sometimes helpful tool.

Introduction and overview

Introduction

Trade models are of tremendous political importance. By pretending to see into the future and putting numbers on the 'welfare gains' accruing from trade liberalisation, such models have provided irresistible ammunition to negotiators, particularly those advocating rapid opening. At the Hong Kong WTO ministerial in December 2005, for instance, the press conferences of major players such as Robert Portman (USA) and Peter Mandelson (EU) were sprinkled with the findings of models, presented as fact. The incessant repetition of benefit numbers in many billions of dollars inevitably puts those advocating a more cautious approach to liberalisation on the defensive, even when such caution is fully warranted (not only by the mixed experience in recent decades of trade liberalisation in practice, but also by the weaknesses of 'typical' computable general equilibrium, or CGE, models, as this paper clearly demonstrates).

In this paper we focus on the simulation models developed at the Global Trade Analysis Project (GTAP) at Purdue University, Indiana, and the LINKAGE project at the World Bank. The reference models share a common intellectual ancestry and associated personnel.[1] The LINKAGE/GTAP models draw heavily on standard international trade theory, essentially a branch of micro-economics. This paper argues that their methodology for calculating the benefits of liberalisation has dubious empirical relevance at best. This problem is exacerbated by the particular specification of trading behaviour that they adopt. We show that there is no reason to take seriously the exact numbers about gains from liberalisation that they churn out, and that their order of magnitude could be estimated without resorting to the computer in any case.

GTAP, LINKAGE, and all other CGE constructs are based on economy-wide data sets and are therefore necessarily 'macro-economic' in nature and have to be analysed in macro-economic terms. However, the models make strong assumptions about the macro-economy and fail to trace through the full economy-wide implications of trade liberalisation.

To understand why this problem arises, consider the tariff increases for steel that the USA imposed in 2002. A strictly 'partial equilibrium' analysis of their impacts would investigate the US steel industry only. Presumably greater protection supporting higher steel prices would enable it to produce more and displace imports. But the price increases would in turn adversely affect the car industry and many other steel-using industries by driving up costs, and this in part would be passed along into higher prices. If imports of goods competing with US products incorporating steel were to rise sharply, there would be visible 'general equilibrium' or macro-economic repercussions. If the exchange rate – the pivotal price in any open economy – were to respond, there would be strong repercussions for the whole system. These would spill over to the rest of the world, and so on.

The standard models fail to trace out fully these macro-economic effects because, to maintain consistency with their micro-economic foundations, they assume that: (i) fixed or 'full' employment of labour and capital is maintained everywhere in the world as a consequence of (ii) movements in industry cost structures, which are complicated and difficult to trace; (iii) each country's trade deficit (or surplus) stays constant after liberalisation; and (iv) completely flexible taxes on households enable each country's internal economy to adjust smoothly. In other words, the GTAP/LINKAGE models are designed to assume that 'the price system' will always respond to liberalisation in such a way as to increase overall well-being. But what if the exchange rate doesn't respond, because it is driven by events in financial markets and not by trade? Or the trade deficit widens after liberalisation? Or unemployment goes up? In developing countries which have historically suffered from large trade deficits, significant debt problems, and a large informal economy with underemployment in modern sectors, these are pressing policy concerns that any trade model needs to address.

In this paper we explain the inadequacies of standard CGE models by submitting them to scrutiny at both the micro and the macro level. Comparisons and contrasts between trade theory and open economy macro-economics are brought in where appropriate. We concentrate on liberalisation of the agricultural sector in the context of the Doha Round and work on an illustrative two-region, three-sector model, using GTAP numbers. In this manner we study the effects on each region and sector of tariff and subsidy reductions in a framework that is relatively easy to manipulate and understand. The two regions in our model are sub-Saharan Africa (SSA) and the rest of the world (ROW). We did not see a great deal of benefit in diving into the full complexity of, for example, the GTAP 6 (2005) global database (which encompasses 57 production sectors in 87 countries/regions). Our model is a stylised condensation of the World Bank constructs. As such, it suffices to deal with the methodological issues we present.

Overview

The paper is separated into two parts. In Part I, we present an analytical critique of CGE models, starting with a scrutiny of their micro-economic foundations, before moving on to examine their macro-economics. In Part II, we use a table-top two-region and three-sector CGE model which represents sub-Saharan Africa (SSA) and the rest of the world (ROW). With this model we show that when alternative (and arguably more plausible) assumptions are made, the expected results of trade liberalisation are radically changed.

The paper starts with a review of standard approaches to calculating the 'gains from trade' that liberalisation is said to generate. A critique of the micro-economic assumptions underlying standard 'little triangle' welfare estimates is presented, which reveals the huge assumptions that underlie this method of calculating welfare. We also show that, despite all the fanfare, the magnitude of the welfare gain produced by the models is small relative to GDP, and that the purported impact on poverty is small compared with the number of poor people in the world.

We explain the 'Armington' specifications of foreign trade incorporated into the GTAP/LINKAGE models. We show that the fiscal (or 'income') effect generated by the Armington specifications shifts the total real spending of consumers when tariffs or subsidies are altered (the cause of this macro-economic effect is explained in detail). We show why this effect runs counter to the micro-economic foundations for welfare computations, which presuppose that spending adjusts only in response to sector-specific price adjustments.

We then provide an explanation of how the GTAP/LINKAGE models work in a closed economy. We explain the underlying causality assumptions present in the World Bank GTAP/LINKAGE models and show how alternative Keynesian causality assumptions might be introduced into such models. We go on to open up the analysis to foreign trade with Armington specifications and explain how the flow of funds and exchange rates are conceptualised in the World Bank model. Here we contrast the micro-economics-based formulation of most trade models with an open-economy macro-economic specification explicitly incorporating the exchange rate.

The first key point is that one must select a macro causal scheme (or 'closure') to impose on any model. World Bank models almost invariably assume that inputs of primary resources are fixed, which means that in effect there is full employment. They also presuppose that the government deficit is fixed, which implies that direct taxes on households must be endogenous. In particular, if import tariffs or export subsidies are changed, then direct taxes must adjust to compensate for the altered revenue flows. There is also a fixed external deficit, and saving-determined capital formation.

The second key point is that standard models make implausible assumptions about the real changes in exchange rates, in effect making the exchange rate a mechanism for achieving their results. However, there is no reason to expect the exchange rate in any actual economy to behave in the way the model thinks it should.

The final section of Part I explains how the Armington trade specification creates an inconsistency in the welfare calculation of CGE models. Applied CGE models try to adopt an 'elasticities' approach to the analysis of liberalisation, in contrast with a more Keynesian 'absorption' analysis. But because of the way that the Armington trade specification and the fiscal balance scenario built into the models interact, they inadvertently also practise absorption macro-economics as well. The interaction creates a fiscal adjustment effect, which introduces the biases in welfare calculations explained above. To the best of our knowledge, this bias has not previously been identified. Fortunately for World Bank modellers, who tend to use high elasticity estimates,[2] the fiscal effect and therefore the bias becomes weaker when 'Armington elasticities' are higher.

In Part II of the paper we present an alternative model to that of the World Bank. The goal and scope of our model is essentially to reduce dimensionality and simplify where possible in order to (i) show in simplified terms how LINKAGE models work, and (ii) show how changes in causality assumptions can affect results in models like LINKAGE. We provide a detailed comparison of our model with that of the World Bank. In our model, we run simulations using two different causality assumptions. In our first set of simulations, we make causality assumptions that are very close to those used in the World Bank's LINKAGE model. In our second set of simulations, we use an alternative set of causalities that rely heavily on Keynesian, arguably more realistic, assumptions.[3] In each set of simulations we present various liberalisation scenarios, starting with a simple, single tariff removal in Africa, up to radical liberalisation and a 'likely' Doha outcome. By reporting simulation results under different causality assumptions and different parameter regimes we considerably broaden the policy maker's horizon.

We then present the results of these different simulations. A key result is that the causality assumptions determine simulation results. Thus endogenising the government deficit produces completely different results from those produced when it is left constant. We show that while the World Bank's assumptions continually generate 'gains from trade' after a liberalisation, the Keynesian assumptions suggest the potentially great risk of macro-economic instability in developing economies. Given that there is no consensus in economics as to which set of assumptions is more plausible, we conclude that developing countries would be ill advised to follow the radical recommendations of the World Bank's liberalisation strategy insofar as it rests on results drawn from the current trade models.

The paper ends with two sets of conclusions, one regarding the critique of CGE (and especially World Bank) modelling of trade liberalisation, and the other concerning current WTO liberalisation negotiations.

Part I: CGE Models of Trade Liberalisation in Practice

In Part I we present an analytical critique of the CGE models of the sort used by the GTAP (Purdue University) and LINKAGE (World Bank) projects, starting with a scrutiny of their micro-economic foundations, before moving on to examine their macro-economics.

Micro-economic foundations

In this section we review standard approaches to calculating the 'gains from trade' that liberalisation is said to generate. A critique of the micro-economic assumptions underlying standard 'little triangle' welfare estimates is presented, which reveals the huge assumptions that underlie this method of calculating welfare. We also show that despite all the fanfare, the magnitude of the welfare gain produced by the models is small relative to GDP, and that the purported impact on poverty is small compared with the number of poor people in the world.

Welfare calculations

'Utopian capitalism' (a phrase coined by the environmental philosopher Mark Sagoff in 1988) is a good label for the micro-economic approach to well-being that lies at the core of mainstream models. It assumes that all resources are fully employed, that consumers are all quite similar and behave in a fully rational fashion, and that arbitrage opportunities have been exploited so that prices for the same product in different places and at different times are the same (after correction for transport and storage costs, and so on).

In slightly fancier language, because of price arbitrage, the cost at the margin of producing a good or commodity is usually equal to the marginal well-being that its consumption generates. In the absence of any 'distortions', which prevent full price arbitrage, the economy achieves 'Pareto optimality', and welfare is maximised.

The real world, according to the 'Utopian capitalism' view, does have a few distortions, mostly due to state intervention. In the context of trade liberalisation models, 'distortions' are taken to be tariffs on imports and exports (or 'tariff-equivalents' of exchange controls, quotas, and other 'non-market' restrictions) or production subsidies. The question that the CGE trade models seek to answer is 'how much would well-being or welfare rise if distortions such as tariffs were removed?'.

Calculations of welfare in CGE models rely on extremely stringent assumptions, which make such calculations highly dubious. First, CGE models assume that groups of consumers and groups of producers behave essentially in similar ways. The standard methodology for conceptualising 'consumer surplus' as a social benefit was proposed in the first half of the nineteenth century by French engineer-economists such as Jules Dupuit (1844). Figure 1 illustrates the argument. A bridge has just been constructed and it is intended to levy a toll P_C per crossing (presumably collected over a number of years) to cover its costs. The assessment of consumer surplus depends on a series of hypothetical calculations. If a very high toll is levied, there would be a very small number of crossings, as indicated by the vertical bar to the far left of the diagram. A somewhat lower price would induce more people to cross, as indicated by the two leftmost bars, and so on.

Figure 1: The original idea of consumer surplus: Dupuit's bridge model

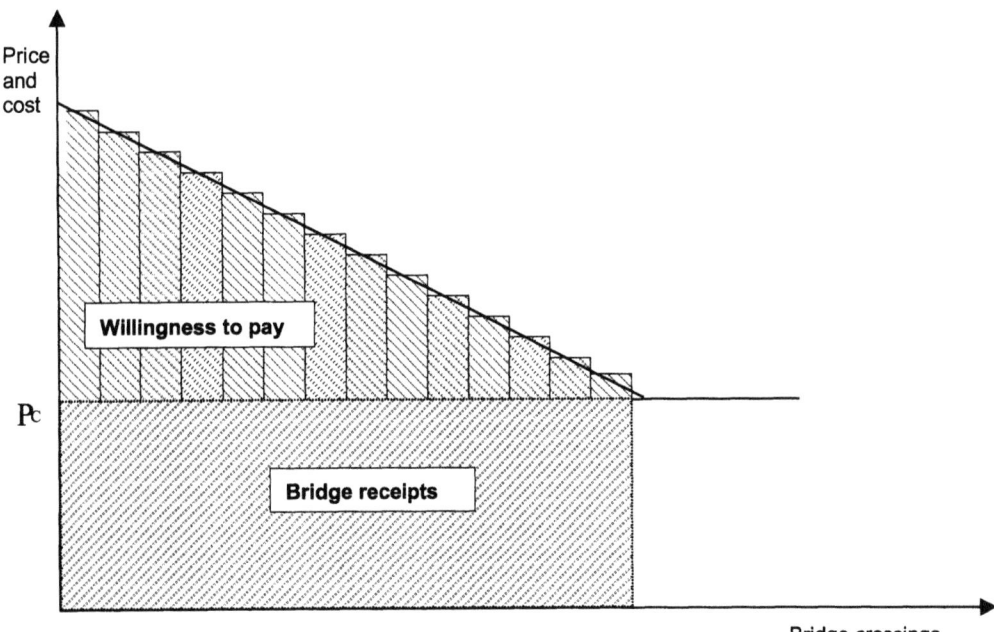

The area covered by all the vertical bars until the toll falls to P_C represents the total 'willingness to pay' of everyone who wants to cross at that cost. The more-or-less triangular shaded area is Dupuit's proposed measure of the total benefit to consumers from building the bridge.

Note that we are talking about *different* people crossing the bridge here: those who are willing to pay a lot, then those who would pay a bit less, and so on. This pricing scheme is the one a discriminating monopolist could use to extract maximum 'surplus' from its customers. As such, there is a big informational problem in extracting the data to plot the curve.

Figure 2 illustrates the contemporary version of this approach, as a 'deadweight loss' calculation characteristic of 'Utopian capitalism', in which consumers are presumed to be essentially the same. Figure 2 illustrates how distortions such as taxes or tariffs are understood to reduce welfare. In an undistorted market for a single product with the usual demand and supply curves, P^* would be the equilibrium price and Q^* the quantity produced and consumed. If the government imposed a sales tax, production would be driven down to Q_S. The price that consumers pay would rise to P_D and producers would receive just P_S per unit sold. The shaded rectangle shows the breakdown of tax receipts between lower 'consumer surplus' (measured by the area under the demand curve) and lower revenue for producers.

Figure 2: 'Little triangles' showing the calculation of the deadweight loss after the imposition of a tariff

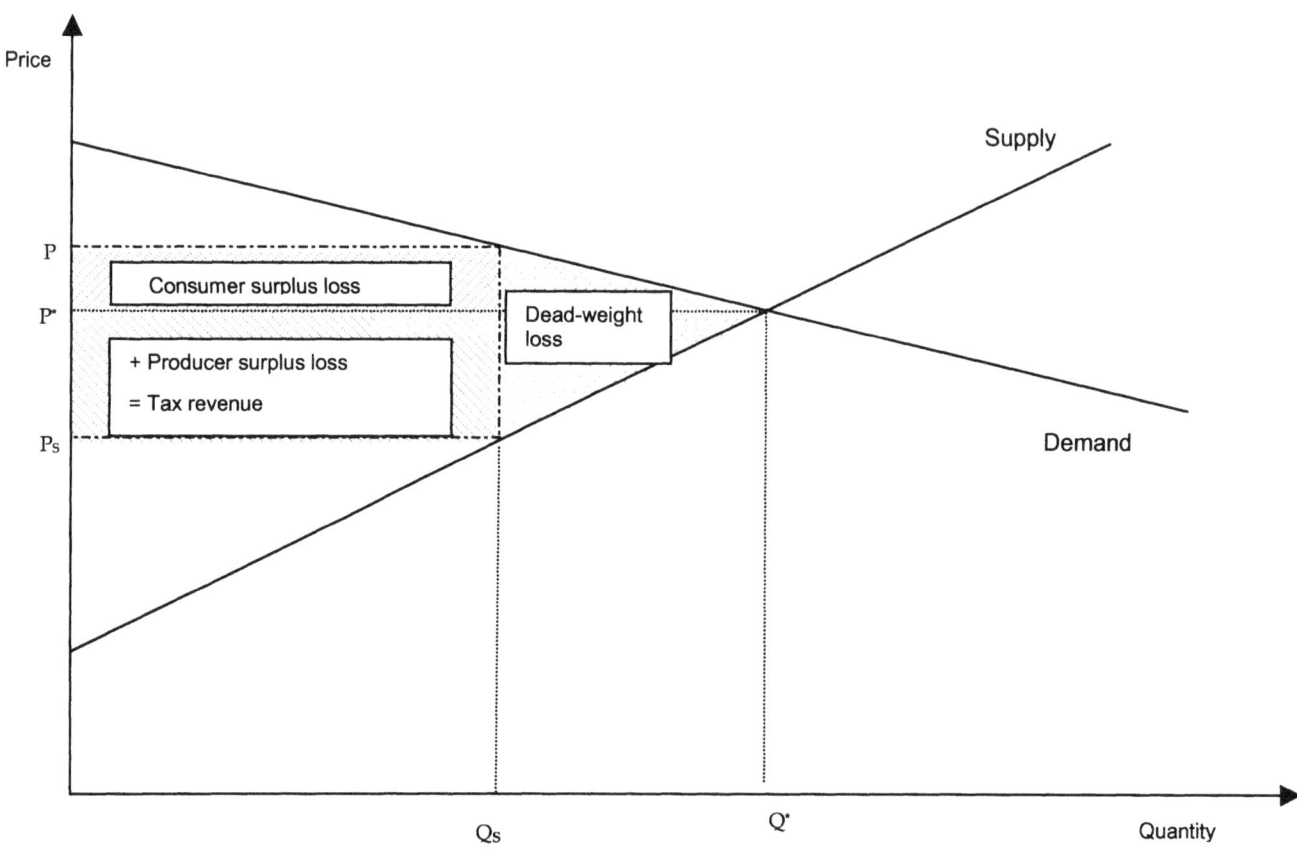

So far the private sector's loss is the government's gain. But there is also a 'little triangle' to the right of Q_S between the demand and supply curves which, in the Utopian capitalist view, measures the welfare caused by imposing the tax. Removing the tax would evidently produce a similar gain. In micro-economic terms, imposing a tariff creates a similar 'deadweight loss'. The basis for the CGE trade models used by the World Bank is that the liberalisation of trade would remove distortions and result in welfare gains. CGE modellers set out to calculate the size of little triangles, and hence the welfare gains, from liberalising trade. This is done in practice by estimating the levels and slopes of the demand and supply curves in Figure 2 from market data.

The distributive basis of Figure 2 is not the same as Dupuit's. Figure 2 assumes that demand, and possibly supply, result from many individual decisions. The only possible rationale is that consumers and producers as groups behave essentially alike. If they did not, then one would have to go back to differential pricing along the lines of Dupuit's bridge authority to identify beneficiaries by individual willingness to pay. The assumption that 'economic agents' are very similar is central to Utopian capitalism. Does this hypothesis make sense?

There are at least two levels at which this question might be posed. In the data, are firms and households in any single economy 'broadly similar' in terms of structure, per capita income level, and so on? How similar are the national economies that enter into a global model? As discussed in Appendix 1, even a cursory look at the numbers shows that, for both national and world economies, dissimilarity is the rule.

Secondly, can micro-economic theory provide plausible justifications for the use of little triangle calculations? Three examples can be mentioned in this context, each one less appealing than the next.

One example is that the economy behaves as if it were Robinson Crusoe's (without Friday and associates), or in fancy terminology that it is controlled by a 'representative agent'. A typical sufficient condition for a representative agent is that every consumer has an income elasticity of demand equal to one for every product, and that the income distribution is fixed and independent of prices (Kirman, 1992). These conditions are clearly violated in CGE models. Income elasticities of demand differ for the various types of product, and are certainly less than one for foods ('Engel's Law'). In addition, income distributions change.

Alternatively, one could recognise that consumers and producers do differ in tastes and available technologies, but that a 'social welfare function' exists, which combines individual utility functions into an overall indicator of well-being. If this function is maximised it can underlie an economy-wide demand function. Unfortunately, it isn't clear who or what maximises this function. In any case, the maximisation necessarily would involve setting the income distribution, a highly unlikely event in practice.

Finally, the economy conceivably could arrive at a Pareto optimal position if, after a policy shift, bribes or 'compensation' are (or could or should be) paid by winners to losers in order to maximise overall welfare. Divisive political and social judgements about what sorts of payments are acceptable would obviously be required. Moreover, major advocates of liberalisation are sceptical. The Oxford economist Ian Little was the intellectual father of the liberalisation component of the Washington Consensus. Yet his scathing critique still stands: 'It seems improbable that … many people would … be prepared to say that a change which … made the rich so much richer that they could (but would not) overcompensate the poor, who were made poorer, would necessarily increase the wealth of the community' (Little 1957: 90). More recently, the MIT economist Paul Samuelson, an ardent proponent of free trade, pointed out that the compensation criterion is hypocritical: 'Should non-economists accept [the claim that compensations *could* be made to 'buy in' losers] as cogent rebuttal if there is no evidence that compensating fiscal transfers have been made or will be made? Marie Antoinette said, 'Let them eat cake'. But history records no transfer of sugar and flour to her peasant subjects.' (Samuelson 2004: 144).

These three sets of conditions at best have a tenuous connection to the economic world as we know it. Micro-economics in its simple form, with dubious welfare calculations based on such stringent assumptions, obviously has serious limitations as the method of choice for calculating gains from trade liberalisation. Ironically, it is precisely the focus on this dubious measure that diverts attention from possibly more relevant measures of liberalisation outcomes, such as the current account and employment indicators usually held constant by World Bank analysts. The usage of the term 'welfare gains' in the public debate implies (at least for non-economists, if not also for some of our micro-oriented colleagues) a certain ideal universality, as if a higher number for welfare would imply an improvement in the general well-being of individuals. As the preceding discussion shows, this is clearly not the case.

More on triangles

Even if the welfare assumptions did make sense, if Utopian capitalism existed, or winners compensated losers, it is difficult in practice to calculate precise welfare gains. Additionally, specific gains can be manipulated by clever modellers. The gains can be made to be 0.2 per cent or 0.7 per cent or 1.9 per cent by suitable choices of 'elasticities' and other parameters. Since elasticities are a measure of the 'slope' of demand and supply curves, higher elasticities 'flatten' the demand and supply curves used in Figure 2 and make the area of the little triangle larger.

Much of the debate in the literature on trade modelling is over the elasticities and other parameters that should be used. However, econometric and other statistical procedures cannot narrow the range of parameter values sufficiently to decide between one story or another, – because there is too much 'noise' in the data. The parameters used to estimate the gains in recent Doha models are no exception. These have continually been challenged and the estimated welfare gains in recent Doha models have been shrinking over time, as emphasised by Ackerman (2005). In 2002 a GTAP study reported $254bn[4] of benefits for the world from complete liberalisation and $108bn for developing countries. The estimates for 2005 shrank to $84bn and $22bn respectively. Simulations for the sorts of tariff reductions being contemplated for the Doha Round reduce these estimated welfare gains by around two-thirds, more for developing countries.

All these arguments about elasticities need to be put in perspective. One can safely assert *a priori* that the estimates of welfare gains from full trade liberalisation will be somewhere in the vicinity of -0.5 per cent to +2–3 per cent, depending on the choice of elasticities. Attempts to quantify welfare gains and losses in the manner described above began almost 50 years ago (Harberger 1959).[5] Ever since, with standard specifications of demand and supply curves, the inevitable result has been that the benefits amount to at most a few per cent and more often a fraction of one per cent of the value of output. Intuitively this is apparent when looking at the area of the triangle, which is always small in comparison to the 'big rectangles' representing tax receipts and the value of output. Not surprisingly, gains from liberalising trade in World Bank models often come out in the 0–1 per cent range in comparison with world GDP. When it is guaranteed *a priori* that such gains will be small, why bother?

Moreover, we do not live in Utopia. Vested interests have ways to protect themselves. In a 'Trade Note', Anderson and Martin (2005) assert that '[I]f members succumb to the political temptation to put limits on tariff cuts for the most sensitive farm products, much of the prospective gain from Doha could evaporate. Even if only 2 per cent of HS6 agricultural tariff lines in developed countries are classified as sensitive (and 4 per cent in developing countries, to incorporate also their 'Special Products' demand), and are thereby subject to just a 15 per cent tariff cut (as a substitute for the TRQ [Tariff Rate Quotas] expansion mentioned in the Framework Agreement), the welfare gains from global agricultural reform would shrink by three-quarters.'

More recently, trade negotiation observers have reported that WTO members 'remain divided on both the number of products that they should be allowed to classify as 'sensitive' and precisely how to expand TRQs for them. These are both crucial to the overall negotiations: many governments estimate that as few as 20–50 tariff lines could account for virtually all of their agricultural exports to major markets.'[6] Thus, the benefit-*reducing* impact of such exemptions is likely to be much stronger on developing countries with undiversified economies that rely heavily on a few primary commodity exports. Small portions of little triangles represent the negligible welfare gains that would be left.

Measuring the poverty impact

The 'poverty impact' of trade liberalisation is often similarly overstated. Placed in perspective, the results are depressing. In addition, the mechanism through which this impact is estimated is mechanistic and crude. The standard approach to estimating the effects of liberalisation on the poor is via a 'poverty elasticity' that is supposed to measure the percentage decrease in a 'headcount ratio' (the share of the population with income below an absolute poverty line, such as $2 per day) that would result from a one per cent increase in (say, low-wage) income. These elasticities range from fractional values to two or three, depending on the country, sector, or time period under consideration. The World Bank prefers to run its LINKAGE projections out to 2015. By then, Doha-style liberalisation would reduce the number of poor people (defined by a $2 per day poverty line) by a mere six million out of a global total of 1,946 million living below the poverty line!

Operational model details

In this section we begin to explain how the models work, beginning with the 'Armington' specifications of foreign trade incorporated in GTAP, LINKAGE, and almost all other CGE trade models. We show that the 'fiscal' (or 'income') effect generated by the Armington specifications runs counter to the models' micro-economic foundations for welfare computations, creating internal biases and making the calculations meaningless.

Armington trade

There is a Gothic quality to World Bank CGE model architecture. The great cathedrals have simple floor plans (like Figure 2), but with their arches, towers, gargoyles, spandrels, and stained glass they are immensely complicated structures. Mainstream trade modellers have spent the past three decades adding similar features to a basically simple model, making their constructs extremely difficult to understand. Much ornamentation comes from the 'Armington' specification of foreign trade, as described in this section.

To see how the modelling works, we have to examine the details of the trade accounts in the World Bank/GTAP specification. In general, trade theorists (and modellers) distinguish between intermediate imports and final imports. The Armington set-up operationalises multi-lateral trade of final goods, in the sense that it solves the problem of determining origin and destination of any country's imports and exports of, say, tomatoes.[7] An important assumption often built into the standard CGE models is that intermediate imports are non-competitive.[8] Another assumption is that final imports are 'imperfectly competitive'.[9] Armington (1969) suggested a trick for making home and foreign goods imperfect substitutes so that if the price of one sort of product goes down, more of it will be consumed (and less of the other product will be consumed) but there will not be complete substitution. The strength of the response is gauged by an 'elasticity of substitution', which is discussed at length below.

The reason why 'Armington' assumptions are made is that perfectly competitive imports, where goods sourced from home and abroad are indistinguishable, do not fit easily with what happens in the real world. The logical conclusion of assuming perfectly competitive imports is that rational consumers would buy goods from the cheapest source exclusively, so that trading economies in a multi-country, multi-commodity world would end up being specialised in the commodities they produced the most cheaply. Such extreme behaviour is not observed in reality.

Stanford (1992) gives careful consideration to the plausibility of the Armington specifications. On the surface, they appear to provide a fairly simple operational model structure for trade. It seems reasonable that an individual household in the USA might decide to buy a typical 'American' or 'foreign' car. However, the *national* product differentiation integral to the Armington specifications ignores the fact that companies, not countries, increasingly determine the characteristics of products. A Toyota car manufactured in Japan is identical to the same model made in the USA, and the Toyota Group itself decides how much international trade to undertake. In other words, much international trade is intra-company, which makes the Armington set-up irrelevant.

Although the justification for adopting Armington specifications is questionable, with little empirical back up, hard-core CGE modellers go a step further and sub-divide or 'nest' categories of imports and exports (not to mention production inputs such as land and various labour skill categories, components of the consumption basket, and so on) up to three levels or more of disaggregation to 'describe' their substitution possibilities in fine detail. For example, intra- and extra-regional imports might trade off to generate an 'overall' import category, which would then substitute with domestic goods.[10] Or maybe the category nesting should go the other way. Substitution possibilities abound in this line of Gothic architecture, making it all the more difficult to penetrate what is going on.

Armington trade and welfare calculations

Leaving aside questions of plausibility, the most important implication of the Armington technique is that it introduces a fiscal bias, which severely undermines the welfare calculations of the World Bank models themselves. The details of how the fiscal bias arises are explained on page 21 and following, where the model is carefully set out. Here we explain why it undermines the models' welfare calculations.

The traditional measure of welfare gains is based on movements of prices and quantities along demand and supply curves, which are 'substitution effects'. The curves themselves do not move when a tax or tariff is adjusted; there are no 'income effects'. However, we show that due to the interaction between the Armington assumption and the fiscal specification of the models, macro repercussions do shift the schedules in GTAP and LINKAGE, stimulating unavoidable income effects and thereby creating a systemic bias of unknown direction and magnitude in the estimates of welfare changes.

For example, built into the World Bank's LINKAGE model is the assumption that when government revenue falls due to a reduction in tariffs, taxes on household consumption automatically increase to drive the government deficit back down to its original level. As will be discussed below, the negative *direct* impact of a higher tax on aggregate real consumption is greater than the positive *indirect* effect of tariff reduction via a lower price. When effective demand declines as a consequence, then so must sectoral consumption levels, and this income effect shrinks the little triangles. Of course, many other things are going on in a CGE solution that can offset such causal chains, but our simulations with a small model in Part II suggest that income effects are quite important (especially when elasticities take on more 'reasonable' values than the Bank is wont to stipulate).

Model specification and macro causality in a closed economy

Here we lay the closed economy foundations necessary for the open economy discussion of LINKAGE/GTAP-type models and alternatives in the following sections.

Analysing the structure of costs and prices is the best way to understand how a CGE model operates.[11] The continuo line in neoclassical economics is that prices adjust to clear markets in such a way as to maximise welfare. If only the government did not impose taxes, welfare would be as good as it could be in the market depicted in Figure 2. However, individual market clearing for *goods* is distinctly *not* the case in CGE models. Rather, changes in prices of *factors* (wages and profit rates) permit the full employment of labour and capital that mainstream models postulate. To see how this scenario of largely delinked CGE price and quantity relationships plays out, it is simplest first to consider an economy closed to foreign trade. This economy, in fact, is very similar to the one Keynes (1936) described in Chapter 19 of his *General Theory*.[12]

In any productive sector the value of output is the sum of production costs. In the simplest case one can think just of capital and labour inputs:[13]

$$PX = wL + rK \text{ or } 1 = \omega(L/X) + \rho(K/X). \tag{C}$$

Production costs equal wages plus profits. 'Wages' are the product of the wage rate and employment; 'profits' are the profit rate multiplied by the capital stock. In the equation on the left, X is real output, P its price, w the nominal wage, L employment, r the profit rate, and K is capital employed. In the second equation, $\omega = w/P$ and $\rho = r/P$ are the 'real' wage and profit rates.[14]

Suppose for the moment that w and r are set by institutional considerations. If the managers running firms more or less minimise costs, their actions will give rise to a behavioural 'cost function' tying P to input costs w and r:

$$P = P(w,r). \tag{CF}$$

The firm passes per unit labour and capital costs into the price of its output.

In World Bank models, mathematical functions used to represent $P(w,r)$ are almost always given a specific algebraic form involving a 'constant elasticity of substitution' (CES).[15] In the present context, the 'elasticity' is a parameter indicating how aggressively a firm would use more capital and less labour to produce a given level of output if the factor cost ratio ω/ρ happened to rise. A 'high' elasticity (say with a value exceeding unity) means that the L/K ratio would decrease 'a lot'.

Many other algebraic specifications for cost functions have been proposed, and there is no obvious empirical reason to choose one over the other. However, a CES function is easy to manipulate mathematically and can be readily extended to permit 'nesting' of substitution possibilities.

In a multi-sectoral framework, the price in each sector will be set by such a function. If labour and capital can switch between sectors so that competition leads to uniform wages and profits all round, then an individual price P_s cannot vary freely to clear the market in its sector s. If it did, then that sector's producers would be forced off their cost function, which determines P_s from the 'macro prices' w and r. In other words, specifying sectoral cost functions means that 'market-clearing prices' cannot exist at the industry level. In such models, all sector-level prices move against one another in response only to wage and profit changes. In a model based on open-economy macro-economics, bringing in an Armington-style international trade specification will loosen this price rigidity, but not by very much.

According to a piece of micro theory that Keynes called the 'second classical postulate' and that contemporary economists call 'Shepherd's Lemma', cost minimisation by firms means that input-output ratios for labour and capital will depend on the real factor prices introduced above:[16]

$$L/X = \lambda(\omega,\rho) \text{ and } K/X = \kappa(\omega,\rho). \tag{SL}$$

Although they long ago went on to other concerns, micro-economic theorists put a lot of effort into working out the implications of Shepherd's Lemma at the time when CGE models were being born. Since then, applied modellers have concentrated mostly on adding spandrels and gargoyles fashioned from extensions of equations (CF) and (SL).

Equations (C) through (SL) state that the output price P and input-output ratios L/X and K/X depend on w and r via the real factor prices $\omega = w/P$ and $\rho = r/P$. The same logic applies to many sectors in which case X and P are 'vectors' or lists of output and price levels.

Now come a few implications (for simplicity stated at the one-sector level):

Levels of employment of labour L and capital K will be given by the input coefficients from (SL) multiplied by output levels X (if there are many sectors, total employment levels are just the sectoral sums).

Multiplying L/X by X and w and K/X by X and r gives wage and profit incomes $Y_w = wL$ and $Y_r = rK$ (or sums across sectors).

The value of consumption PC is the portion of income flows not taxed away or saved (or paid out as net interest in a more realistic specification). It can be written as

$$PC = (1-s_w)Y_w + (1-s_r)Y_r - PT$$

in which T is a real 'non-distorting lump-sum' direct consumption tax assumed to be extracted from household spending flows, and s_w and s_r are saving rates from wage and profit income.[17]

Real consumption C is

$$C = (1-s_w)(Y_w/P) + (1-s_r)(Y_r/P) - T.$$

A change in T impacts on C one-for-one, a twist that will turn out to be important in understanding LINKAGE fiscal economics.

After taking into account the definitions of wage and profit incomes, this second version of the consumption function makes C an algebraic function of output X: $C = C(X)$. More output leads to more consumption but also to higher nominal ($S = s_w Y_w + s_r Y_r$) and real (S/P) savings as well.

A 'material balance' or description of the uses of real output takes the form

$$C(X) + I + G - X = 0 \tag{MB}$$

in which I is investment in the national income and product (NIPA) sense of 'gross fixed capital formation' and G is real government spending on goods and services. All sources of effective demand add up to determine output.

If I and G are respectively determined by companies' investment decisions and public policy, then equation (MB) can be solved for X. The price system does enter into output determination by influencing levels of real income Y_w/P and Y_r/P but apart from that there is no close linkage between output and prices in a Keynesian economic world. In a closed economy Keynesian model then, the demand injections I and G are pre-determined, and nominal government revenue will be set by tax policy (making real revenue T a function of X) and the level of economic activity.

World Bank/GTAP models incorporate a different macro scenario than the Keynesian model. In accordance with 'Say's Law' which asserts that all resources are fully employed, they stipulate that both labour and capital are fully employed. (Although they habitually use the word 'fixed' in place of 'full,' mainstream CGE models postulate full employment of labour and capital). We need a fixed nominal variable called a *numeraire* to scale the price system, and it is convenient to retain the wage rate w. The profit rate r can be assumed to adjust to bring the demand for capital into equality with the available supply. In a model in which there are no 'black holes' in the accounting (as at present), demand for labour will then equilibrate to supply as well.[18] Real factor prices ω and ρ can be viewed as adjusting to clear their respective markets. The price system will reconfigure accordingly and income levels Y_w and Y_r will be determined from the supply side.

Which scenario is more realistic? For the moment we can beg the question, but it does suggest that more than one macro causal structure should be borne in mind when playing with CGEs. In the literature, causality issues are discussed under the rubric of model 'closure'. World Bank publications recognise that doubts about specific closures may exist and are explicit about the macro causal schemes of their own models. They just do not deign to present alternatives. Concerns about this form of lopsidedness rarely surface in policy consultations with developing countries or in the public debate.[19]

Open economy (Armington) macro-economics

In this section we explain the basic open economy macro-economics of CGE models. We have not found a coherent discussion of a two-country Armington model in the literature. What follows should be recognised as our own attempt at creating one. With one exception, the results are not surprising in the context of open economy analysis as this already existed half a century ago. However, it makes sense to think them through.

We use a simplified two-country model (sub-Saharan Africa [SSA] and the rest of the world [ROW]), which captures the essence of the LINKAGE/GTAP model without its daunting size. Data was sourced from the GTAP database. Data manipulation was involved (in part due to deficiencies in the sources) but the numbers, as presented in a social accounting matrix (SAM) in Appendix 1, are perhaps representative of the production and trade patterns of the defined regions early in the present decade. As the model is explained, we provide a critique of the assumptions made in the GTAP/LINKAGE specifications.

Flow of funds

The flows of funds are a skeleton key to the macro-economics of any open economy model. To open the lock with simple algebra we can consider the model from the perspective of sub-Saharan Africa and examine the accounts of the private sector, government, and the rest of the world.[20]

For the private sector let I = the value (price x quantity) of investment, S = the value of saving, and L = new loans to the government. Then the private flow of funds is

$$S - I - L = 0. \tag{P}$$

It is also true that private sector net borrowing = increase in financial liabilities minus increase in financial assets = $I - S$. Anyone who invests more than they save has to be a net borrower.

For the government, let G = value of expenditure, R = total net revenue (taxes and tariffs less subsidies), and Δ = aid inflow from abroad. Government saving is $R - G$ so the flow of funds (involving only 'sources') is

$$(R - G) + L + \Delta = 0 \tag{G}$$

in which $R - G < 0$. Government net borrowing is $G - R$, made up of new loans from the private sector and, in the two-country model, ROW.

Since SSA runs a trade deficit, with imports exceeding exports, it has to finance its external imbalance by borrowing or by obtaining a financial transfer from somewhere. In a two-country world the only possibility for this is ROW. Net borrowing from the ROW private sector (or government) is $M - E$ where E = value of SSA exports and M = value of imports.

There are no other net borrowing flows in the system. Because one actor's borrowing must be met by other actor's lending, the sum of net borrowing flows must be zero:

$$(I - S) + (G - R) + (E - M) = 0. \qquad (M)$$

Equation (M) is the basic balance condition in any open economy macro model. Combining it with (P) and (G) and a bit of algebra shows that

$$(M - E) - \Delta = 0 \qquad (F)$$

is the external flow of funds. The SSA trade deficit is covered by ROW's foreign aid.

Before turning to how macro-economics in this system works out, we should slightly restate the flow of funds accounts. The equations above were set up in 'value' terms but for clarity they should be rewritten recognising that *value* is the product of *price* and *quantity*. Anticipating the algebra of Armington imports introduced in the following section, we use national 'supply prices' Z and Z^* respectively for SSA and ROW. Definitions of Z and Z^* are presented below.

The private sector flow of funds (P) becomes

$$S - ZI - L = 0 \qquad (P')$$

in which ZI is the value of real investment at the supply price Z.

The government's flow is

$$(R - ZG) + L + e\Delta^* = 0 \qquad (G')$$

in which the value of net revenue R includes the lump-sum tax ZT (along with tariffs and indirect taxes less subsidies in more complete accounting, which will be important below). The foreign aid inflow in terms of the local currency is $\Delta = e\Delta^*$ in which the ROW government is assumed to set the value of aid in terms of its own currency at Δ^*, and e is the exchange rate.

The value of SSA exports is ZE. To keep symmetry in notation, let the value of SSA imports be $M = eZ^*E^*$ in which E^* is the real ROW export level.[21] Then the external flow of funds can be written as

$$(eZ^*E^* - ZE) - e\Delta^* = 0 \qquad (F')$$

Adding equations (P'), (G') and (F') and switching signs gives

$$(ZI - S) + (ZG - R) + (ZE - eZ^*E^*) = 0 \qquad (M')$$

as the overall macro balance.

In a Keynesian model for a closed economy[22] the demand injections I and G are pre-determined (as explained in the previous section), and nominal government revenue R will be set by tax policy and the level of economic activity. The amount L that the private sector lends to the government follows for (G'). That leaves private saving S as the only variable which can adjust to give equalities in (P') and (M'). Along with consumption ZC, S is an algebraic function of the value of output ZX. There are no *direct* linkages between Z and X. Hence output must vary to make (M') and (P') balance. The saving 'leakage' S and value of output ZX *adjust* to meet the demand injections ZI and ZG. In the Keynesian world, then, real GDP is determined by effective demand, although of course changes in tax rates and other policy variables will affect Z, S, and R with potentially large macro spillovers.

Most World Bank models freeze financial transactions between the private sector and government, setting L to an exogenously fixed value. The full employment assumption sets the saving level so that, from the private flow of funds, the only variable that can possibly adjust in the private sector flow of funds (P') is real investment, I. In World Bank (and most neoclassical) CGE models, investment is determined by saving and fiscal policy. The models also treat the foreign deficit Δ as pre-determined. If government spending G and tariff and subsidy rates are set by policy, the only remaining free variable in (G') is T. In the World Bank models, direct taxes have to adjust endogenously to assure macro-economic balance in (M') at the economy's exogenously specified levels of employment and foreign aid.[23]

These are peculiar assumptions. Such adept fiscal programming is never observed (let alone over 15 years, as assumed in LINKAGE model simulations!). There are many other ways in which economies arrive at macro-economic balance, as discussed in the following sections.

Exchange rates

Before getting into Armington *per se*, recall that the LINKAGE/GTAP models are based on international trade theory. There are important differences in the ways that trade theorists and open-economy macro-economists treat price–cost relationships that are worth emphasising. In trade theory, if Z^* is the border price of imports then their tariff-ridden domestic price is stated as $(1+t)Z^*$. Trade enforces some sort of relationship between the domestic price P of goods that compete with imports and $(1+t)Z^*$. Perfect competition means that the relationship would be

$$P = (1+t)Z^* \qquad \text{(IT)}$$

Armington or other forms of imperfect composition generate other equations tying P to Z^*, as discussed below.

The domestic price P will also decompose into costs, as in equation (CF) above. Suppose that the wage w and profit rate r adjust to bring full employment of labour and capital economy-wide, so that they are pre-determined as far as the cost function for any sector is concerned. Its price is set by its costs. There is *no* reason to expect P from (IT) to come into equality with P from (CF) and no mechanism is immediately available to make that happen.

Of course, mechanisms can be provided. One is to restate equation (CF) as something like

$$P = P(w, r, q) \qquad \text{(CF')}$$

in which q is the cost of an input besides labour and capital that goes into the production of the good whose price is P. The input could be fixed capital (by sector), land, or some specific factor. Then the tariff rate and foreign supply price can determine P in (IT), which in turn determines q in (CF').[24] If B is the quantity of the other input, there will be an income flow qB which will feed into consumption, taxes, and so on.

This approach to price–cost structures is the one that the World Bank adopts in its multi-sectoral CGEs, which contain a plethora of sector-related input prices that can be adjusted to allow determination of final goods prices from foreign prices and tariffs via international trade. The movements of all these input prices are metaphorically viewed as amounting to a shift in the 'real exchange rate'.

In the open-economy macro tradition, the price relationship (IT) is restated as

$$P = e(1+t)Z^* \qquad \text{(OEM)}$$

in which e is the exchange rate that brings P from (OEM) or an Armington variant into equality with P from (CF). The open-economy macro approach is the one used in our simple model. It essentially forces all macro adjustment onto one 'conversion factor' that adjusts to link foreign and domestic prices, rather than having a number of domestic input prices which shift. The final outcomes of the two approaches will not differ greatly, and it is easier to think about movements in one accommodating variable than many.

It is crucial to understand the implications of treating the exchange rate in this manner. The key results of the model depend on shifts in the exchange rate so, for the model to make policy sense, exchange rates in the real world need to behave as the model says they will. There is one thing certain about any economy's real exchange rate. It never follows prevailing ideas about its behaviour over time. Endless effort has been devoted to formulating real exchange rate theories but, in practice, none of them work. A very complicated CGE model will not perform any better than the alternatives, so, at best, its workings have to be interpreted as mapping a possible causal chain. The model's plausibility has become increasingly remote in recent years as exchange rates have been driven far more by forces of finance than those of trade. Even for many developing economies, capital market transactions vastly exceed flows of imports and exports.

Armington open-economy macro-economics

Now we can finally bring in the Armington specification via the supply prices Z and Z^* for SSA and ROW introduced above. What is this 'supply?' The supply in SSA is made up of domestic production and non-intermediate imports.[25] If Z is a price, there has to be a corresponding 'real' Armington aggregate commodity A made up of domestic products and imports so that the total value is ZA.

The value of domestic output is PX. From (OEM), after clearing customs, imports E^* will be worth $e(1+t)Z^*E^*$. The implication is that the value of domestic supply becomes

$$ZA = PX + e(1+t)Z^*E^* \text{ or } 1 = (P/Z)(X/A) + [e(1+t)Z^*/Z](E^*/A) . \quad \text{(A)}$$

We can now apply to (A) the same Shepherd's Lemma bag of tricks employed in connection with (P). A cost function for the supply (or Armington) price Z is[26]

$$Z = Z[P, e(1+t)Z^*] . \quad \text{(Z)}$$

Just who is minimising costs to make this equation hold is never made clear. Whoever the minimiser is, there will be a similar equation for Z^* (including a term in Z/e instead of eZ^*). Armington prices in SSA and ROW mutually impact one another. Each region also depends, via the output price from equation (CF), on its 'own' wage and profit rates as well as the exchange rate (and local tariff rates). In SSA, Z is a highly non-linear weighted average of $w, r, e, t,$ and Z^* (and analogously for Z^* in ROW). Cost minimisation will assure that the 'input ratios' X/A and E^*/A depend on their real (Armington) prices.[27]

Unsurprisingly, the over-determination problem mentioned above reappears in an Armington context. If we drop the exchange rate and turn to trade theory, the two regions' supply price equations boil down to $Z = Z[P(w,r,q),(1+t)Z^*]$ and $Z^* = Z^*[P^*(w^*,r^*,q^*),Z]$. Under World Bank closure assumptions the foreign balance (F') is treated as a binding restriction on any solution to the model. When this solution is disturbed by a change in the tariff rate t (or by changes in the many sectoral tariff rates), for example, external balance has to be restored via shifts in imports and exports in response to adjustments in Z and Z^*. If wages and profit rates are fixed by full employment assumptions, the only way the Armington prices can respond is through changes in the 'other input' prices q and q^*.

In an open economy model the supply price equations contain the exchange rate and become $Z = Z[P(w,r), e(1+t)Z^*]$ and $Z^* = Z^*[P^*(w^*, r^*), Z/e]$, so that e can do the adjusting.

The value of the Armington aggregate ZA will sum to components of demand. That is,

$$ZC(X) + ZI + ZG + ZE - ZA = 0 \qquad \text{(MB')}$$

and we can get a 'material balance' in terms of real output by dividing through by Z.

As just noted, the Armington specification makes the input ratios X/A and E^*/A functions of relative prices. Dividing one expression by the other gives the import/output ratio. We can rewrite the external flow of funds balance (F') as

$$eZ^*\mu[P/e(1+t)Z^*]X - Z\mu^*[P^*e/Z(1+t^*)]X^* - e\Delta^* = 0 \qquad \text{(BP)}$$

in which μ and μ^* are price-dependent ratios of imports to output levels in the two regions.[28] Devaluation or an *increase* in the exchange rate e will reduce the home import coefficient μ and raise the foreign μ^*. As noted above, in a model based in trade theory, Z and Z^* (and q and q^*) would be the adjusting prices.

Now we can do LINKAGE-style open-economy macro, assuming that ROW sets the level of aid Δ^* in terms of its own currency and (like the USA) makes no policy reaction to shifts in the exchange rate. A natural *numeraire* is the ROW wage rate w^*.

In SSA, w and r are supposed to adjust to make demand equal to supply for labour and capital respectively, and r^* is assumed do the same for ROW capital. Shifts in the exchange rate will modify import levels in (BP), so presumably e can vary to clear the balance of payments. After all this has happened, demand for ROW labour will automatically adjust to meet a fixed supply.

Liberalisation in Armington open-economy macro

An obvious question is what consequences will there be if SSA cuts its tariffs.

Presumably imports will increase as μ shifts upward in (BP). There are several channels via which the trade deficit can be brought back to equality with $e\Delta^*$ if t is reduced. One is exchange rate devaluation or an increase in e, which should shift μ back downward and also cause the ROW import coefficient μ^* to rise. If the two responses are strong enough, external balance for a given transfer Δ^* will be restored. The Bank likes to emphasise how liberalisation will rearrange trade flows in the direction of exports through the induced devaluation. Of course, this *result is already built into its model.*

More to the macro point, World Bank models seek to adopt the 'elasticities' approach to balance of payments adjustment, which was introduced before the Second World War and was at the height of its popularity around 50 years ago. A more Keynesian approach to the trade balance that also emerged just after the Second World War emphasises changes in 'absorption' of external perturbations. For a given exchange rate, movements in the level of economic activity, as well as foreign transfers and so on, will reallocate production flows and incomes. As we will see shortly, LINKAGE inadvertently builds in an absorption angle as well.

Assuming the exchange rate behaves as the model thinks it should, in elasticities fashion, it can rebalance (BP) if a 'Marshall-Lerner' condition is satisfied. Because of the cross-dependence of Z and Z^* discussed above, a formal statement in the present set-up is incredibly messy, but the lead terms resemble the usual textbook versions. The elasticities of substitution σ and σ^* between domestic output and imports in the SSA and ROW Armington aggregates A and A^* are the key parameters. In the open-economy macro-economics tradition, such elasticities are usually presumed to take values in the range of one to three. Bank models often peg them in the range of three to six and other projections put them even higher.

Perhaps being overly cynical, we can think of two justifications for this. One is that, as we have seen, higher elasticities tend to enhance welfare gains made by eliminating distortions. The other is that in equation (BP) a devaluation or increase in the exchange rate e will reduce the world price Z/e of SSA exports and shift the terms of trade adversely. There are many possible offsets in a multi-sectoral model. Armington prices Z and Z^* interact with one another and there will be movements in relative prices across sectors. Nevertheless, the shift in the terms of trade against SSA will be *stronger*, the *lower* ROW's demand elasticity η^* is, because the demand response to devaluation will be weaker.

So higher elasticities attenuate or even reverse adverse shifts in the terms of trade in response to devaluation. The problem in the context of reducing protection for agriculture is that price elasticities of demand for products from the sector are *low* (indeed often estimated to be less than one). This is the first lesson that politicians and economists who deal with agriculture tend to learn. The implication is that it makes sense to regulate agricultural prices, because their downward excursions in response to transient upswings in supply or downswings in demand are likely to be very large. In the algebra of (BP), adverse shifts in the agricultural terms of trade in response to tariff reductions look almost inevitable for usually accepted elasticity values. Is that why World Bank economists prefer to boost their numbers for η^* from something like 0.5 to five?[29]

There is a great deal of discussion as to whether Bank modellers (not to mention competitors such as Cline, 2004) choose values of Armington elasticities of substitution that are 'too high'. By making substitution between domestic and imported goods more price-responsive, higher elasticities tend to (i) hold relative prices more stable because quantity responses to price changes are stronger and (ii) add weight to the little triangles so that there are greater welfare gains from removing distortions.

The Armington fiscal effect

In this section, we explain how the Armington trade specification creates an inconsistency in the welfare calculation of the CGE models. We show that because of the way that the Armington trade specification and the fiscal balance scenario interact in the models, they inadvertently also practise absorption macro-economics as well. The interaction creates a fiscal adjustment effect, which introduces the biases in welfare calculations explained above.

The cause of the fiscal effect

In the present context, net revenue R in the government's flow of funds (G') is made up of direct taxes and proceeds from import tariffs,

$$R = ZT + teZ^*E^*.$$

In a World Bank closure, the government deficit is fixed, so that with fixed spending and falling tariff revenues the real consumption tax T must rise to hold R constant. As noted above, a rise in T has a strong *direct* impact on reducing real consumption C. Because consumption makes up a large share of aggregate demand, imports will fall as well.[30]

This 'effect' does not appear in the standard open-economy macro literature and so is worth exploring in a bit more detail. It turns out to be a large gargoyle created by the Armington apparatus.

It makes sense to begin with a quick review of the traditional non-Armington story about the effects of tariff changes. We assume that the price P of domestic output comes from the side of costs and output X is set by Say's Law. The value of output is PX, which also equals household income.

Imports E^* have an internal price $e(1+t)Z^*$ in line with equation (OEM) above. Consumers purchase both domestic output and the imports. A minimalist government puts a tariff on imports and gives the returns back to households as an income transfer. If there is no government spending on goods and services and zero investment, then commodity market equilibrium means that output goes to consumption and exports, or

$$PX = PC + PE.$$

The trade balance (at home prices) is

$$e\Delta^* = eZ^*E^* - PE.$$

Substituting for PE in the equation for PX and rearranging gives

$$PC + eZ^*E^* = PX + e\Delta^*. \qquad (T)$$

The value of consumption of domestic goods plus imports at world prices equals the value of output plus the foreign transfer. An import tariff that is refunded has no *income* effect on demand. Bringing in the tariff/transfer procedure described above, it will also be true that

$$PC + e(1+t)Z^*E^* = PX + etZ^*E^* + e\Delta^*.$$

The term etZ^*E^* cancels out on both sides, or the tariff only induces substitution responses between real consumption of domestic goods C and imports E^*. Little triangle welfare gains from reducing t follow directly. The rub is that devaluation or an increase in e would be required to restore the trade balance, which would drive the import price back up and could largely offset the welfare gain.

Now bring in Armington as in the LINKAGE specification, still assuming that the government levies only an import tariff. Working with an Armington supply aggregate A and price Z, the goods and trade balances in current prices become

$$ZA = ZC + ZE$$

and

$$e\Delta^* = eZ^*E^* - ZE$$

respectively.

From (A) above the Armington cost breakdown is

$$ZA = PX + e(1+t)Z^*E^*.$$

The key point is that in this decomposition the tariff cost $e(1+t)Z^*$ is just one component of the Armington price Z (for future reference, let $\zeta = e(1+t)Z^*E^* / ZA$).

Finally, the government's flow of funds is

$$ZT + etZ^*E^* + e\Delta^* = 0$$

with ZT as the value of a direct tax/transfer on households. Combining and rearranging these equations gives

$$C = (P/Z)X - T \qquad (L)$$

for the impact of tariffs on real aggregate consumption.

There are three immediate (or 'impact') consequences of a reduction in the tariff rate:

First, the tax T will increase and cut into consumption according to

$$\frac{dC}{dt} = -\frac{eZ^*E^*}{Z}.$$

Second, the price ratio P/Z will increase according to

$$d(P/Z) = -\frac{Z}{P}\zeta[\frac{t}{1+t}\hat{t} + \hat{e}]$$

in which a 'hat' over a variable denotes its proportional change ($\hat{t} = dt/t$) and ζ is the share of import costs in the Armington aggregate value of supply defined above.[31] By increasing P/Z a lower tariff will stimulate consumption according to

$$\frac{dC}{dt} = (1-\zeta)\frac{eZ^*E^*}{Z}$$

which is *less* in absolute terms than the reduction due to a higher T.

Finally, as discussed above, the exchange rate will have to increase to restore external balance. This will drive P/Z back downward and cut back the rise in C.

Even if the required exchange rate increase is relatively small, the fiscal effect will dominate: cutting tariffs reduces effective demand and shrinks little triangles. This result is stronger if a big devaluation is needed to restore the balance of trade. Besides cutting back on adverse shifts in the terms of trade, higher Armington elasticities interact with fiscal balance to cut back welfare losses or (in a more complicated set-up) enhance gains.

This is a striking result. But it makes sense to think through scenarios with an endogenous fiscal deficit so that the Bank's odd treatment of household taxes does not apply. Then, because tariff reduction cuts prices and eats into government net revenue, it might be expected to stimulate aggregate demand in addition to raising the import coefficient. Various adjustments can ensue. We can trace through examples for SSA, assuming that feedback effects on ROW are relatively weak.

One possibility would be an endogenous post-liberalisation increase in ROW's new loans to SSA in an example of 'aid-for-trade'. In ROW, higher taxes feeding into government revenue or increased government borrowing from the private sector could let capital flows become an accommodating variable responding to a reduction in SSA tariffs. ROW would 'finance' SSA's reduced exports and higher imports resulting from liberalisation with the exchange rate held constant. From a historical perspective, growing post-liberalisation foreign trade deficits accompanied by rising debt levels in a developing country are not an unlikely adjustment scenario. It is, however, excluded by the assumptions about macro-economic causality made at the World Bank.

Alternatively, the SSA exchange, profit, and wage rates could be held constant and investment could be exogenous. Then the SSA external deficit, government borrowing, and output could all change endogenously in a pure 'absorption' scenario.

Illustrative numbers are attached to World Bank and absorption closures in Part II.

Part II: Simulations and Results

In Part II of the paper we present an alternative to the World Bank model in the form of a table-top two-region and three-sector CGE model which represents sub-Saharan Africa and the rest of the world. With this model we show that when other (and arguably more plausible) assumptions about trade liberalisation are made, the predicted outcomes are radically different.

Aim and scope

We had the following aim in mind: the model should stylise the CGE approach to trade and be capable of providing policy insights with regard to the Doha process. To allow for a critique of the LINKAGE framework, the model is based on broadly the same assumptions and theoretical constructs. Furthermore, in order to contrast the World Bank's model with alternatives, we wanted to be able to change some of those assumptions. Bank models in fact allow for these changes, but usually neither different simulation results nor possibly differing policy recommendations are reported.

Two points should be highlighted from the start. First, we used the GTAP version 5 data set,[32] which neither fully incorporates the Uruguay Round implementation period nor deals in any way with preferential trade agreements (as GTAP 6 does). The most recent version is a more precise and detailed data set, and all recent CGE estimates of welfare gains from liberalisation make use of it, but we argue that using GTAP 5 does not unduly limit our results. We provide a critique of the model's theoretical foundations, and do not want to get involved in a discussion about the precise magnitude – 1.1 per cent or 1.3 per cent of GDP – of welfare estimates. GTAP 5 serves our purposes as a base-year data set that GDP depicts trade between a rich region and a poor region with strongly differing economic structures and characteristics.

Secondly, we still wanted to provide policy insights with regard to the Doha process. How could we do that, with an outdated data set? As we will discuss in more detail below, our results mainly concern the *direction* and *volatility* of changes, and not any specific magnitude. Direction and volatility depend crucially on causality assumptions and not on the precision of the data.

Comparing models – our model versus World Bank models

In this section we provide a detailed comparison of our model with that of the World Bank. In the following paragraphs we contrast our model with the Bank model, by juxtaposing excerpts from the Bank's latest technical reference document[33] with brief sketches of our set-up. We also explain how the closure assumptions differ. See Figure 3 for a summary of this comparison.

Figure 3: Comparison of the World Bank's model and our model

Differences		
	LINKAGE	Our 'replica'
Time horizon	Dynamic; liberalisation implementation and adjustment 'stretched' over 15 years	Static
Trade–growth linkage	Endogenous productivity: Liberalisation increases production through assumed positive efficiency effects	None
Countries/regions	87	Two: sub-Saharan Africa (SSA) and the rest of the world (ROW)
Sectors	57	Three: agriculture, manufactures, services
Factors	Five: Unskilled and skilled labour, land, natural resources, and capital	Two: labour and capital
Exchange rate	Not explicitly modelled as a 'macro' price	Explicitly included
Other		Government expenditures exclusively on services Investment expenditures exclusively on industrial goods ROW intermediate imports exclusively intra-regional; SSA intermediate imports exclusively extra-regional
Database	GTAP 6 (2001 base year, includes preferential trade agreements)	GTAP 5 (1997 base year, no preferential trade agreements); tariff data updated based on GTAP 6
Modelling Language	GAMS	Mathematica

Common features		
	LINKAGE	Our 'replica'
Cost (and production) structure	Leontief (fixed coefficients) in intermediates and CES in value added: inputs are not substitutable, whereas factors trade off against each other according to a constant elasticity of substitution.	
Trade structure	Armington (CES): imports and domestic products are imperfect substitutes; the strength of the substitution effect depends on the size of the constant elasticity of substitution.	
Consumption	Linear Expenditure System: consumption of a specific good increases with income and decreases with its price, depending on a set of parameters. Income elasticities are not all equal to one.	

Static versus dynamic

> 'The Linkage Model is a global dynamic computable general equilibrium model (CGE) with a 2001 base year. [...] A recursive framework is used to drive dynamics, with savings-led investment and productivity. The model incorporates adjustment costs in capital markets and trade-responsive endogenous productivity.' (van der Mensbrugghe, 2005)

First of all, our model is static, and computes one-off effects of liberalisation and other perturbations to the data built into the base-year social accounting matrix (SAM). The Bank's model is also essentially static, but it is run over a number of periods ('years') to generate a simulacrum of dynamic change. For example, tariffs are usually phased out over several years to leave room for adjustments in domestic policies as well as agents' behaviour.

More importantly, the World Bank adopts the assumption that an increasing export/output ratio (say, in response to liberalisation with the positive export response that is built into Bank models) raises a sector's labour productivity according to a pre-set elasticity, as usual. This idea is as old as trade theory itself: when autarchy breaks down in a Ricardian world in which comparative advantage determines trade patterns, the resulting specialisation has positive productivity effects. In the classic example, Portugal and Great Britain increase outputs of wine and cloth respectively for given factors and technology, as each concentrates on the commodity it can produce more cheaply.

While most economists agree that such things can happen, it is by no means undisputed that there are positive linkages to growth and welfare. Given the current broad trends in the manufacturing sector in the USA and its imports of manufactures, for example, one might argue that increased trade has eroded the manufacturing base in the USA and consequently forced industries to specialise and 'move up the value chain'. This is consistent with productivity increases on the one hand but with negative effects on employment, distribution, and welfare on the other hand (there are of course many similar examples in semi-industrialised economies, such as Brazil's). In its Doha models, the Bank's treatment of this issue is mechanical and *ad hoc*, so we chose not to pursue it.

Simple versus complex

> 'It features three production archetypes – crops, livestock, and other – a full range of tax instruments, price markups, multiple labour skills, vintage capital, and energy as an input combined with capital ... and incorporates 87 countries/regions, and 57 sectors'. (van der Mensbrugghe, 2005).

A principal difference between LINKAGE and our model is that we attempt to keep things simple. The size of the Bank's model is in the order of 50,000 equations. This level of detail is most impressive, but it makes the heart of the machine impossible to comprehend. Our model has 'only' 125 equations. This reduction means that we aggregate sectors, factors, and regions: we use three sectors (agriculture, manufactures, and services), not 57; two factors (labour and capital), not five; and two regions (sub-Saharan Africa and the rest of the world) instead of 87 as in LINKAGE.

There are certainly important benefits from higher dimensionality. A global reduction in rice tariffs, for example, has a very different impact on Japan than it does on Switzerland. Our model cannot address this issue, as rice prices and production are subsumed in the broad agricultural sector – and, moreover, Japan and Switzerland appear to be the same country. Similarly, the ROW region comprises countries as diverse as Indonesia and France. The Indonesian agricultural sector enters importantly into GDP and employment, whereas the most prominent aspect of France's agricultural sector (leaving aside the 350 cheeses[34] and sundry other products that please the palates of trade negotiators but which neither LINKAGE nor our model can consider) is the high level of protection it enjoys under Europe's Common Agricultural Policy.

The advantage of the simplifications is that our model remains at least to some extent tractable. It also allows us to focus on macro-economic forces which drive micro results, an aspect of the LINKAGE specification which the Bank's publications elide. It stylises trade between a large, rich region and a smaller, poor region and directly addresses the Doha process with its focus on development concerns, as well as the pivotal negotiating areas of agriculture versus non-agricultural market access (NAMA).

Armington specifications

> 'Trade is modeled using nested Armington and production transformation structures to determine bilateral trade flows'. (van der Mensbrugghe, 2005)

Despite all the problems inherent in the Armington approach, our model is based broadly on the same principles as LINKAGE to make it comparable.[35] On the production side, intermediates enter with fixed coefficients. Their 'Leontief technology' presupposes that intermediate inputs, for example steel and semiconductor chips going into machine tools, are required in constant proportions. If its price increases, one input cannot be partially replaced by another. Imported intermediates are subject to the same assumption that has become traditional in CGE modelling.

Labour and capital, however, trade off against one another according to the ubiquitous constant elasticity of substitution (CES) specification. Consistent with standard micro-economic theory, these functions are derived from a unit cost function that determines the overall price level, which is in turn 'dual' to a production function. The Armington trade structure applies the same principles to determine import and export ratios as well as international prices.

Exchange rates

> 'In its standard version, it is a neo-classical model with both factor and goods market clearing.... Closure is identified with two variables – government savings and foreign capital flows. Both are assumed fixed in any given time period. In the case of the former, direct taxes adjust to meet the fiscal target. In the case of the latter, the real exchange rate adjusts to match the balance of payments constraint'. (van der Mensbrugghe, 2005, p.51)

As pointed out in Part I, the Bank's reference to the exchange rate is disingenuous. LINKAGE does not include exchange rate variables *per se*, and 'exchange rate changes' are a metaphor for thousands of individual price adjustments that are impossible to think through in detail. Our specification explicitly incorporates the exchange rate. The Bank's hidden exchange rates and our visible exchange rates are supposed to accommodate changes in trade flows such that the current account remains constant. How realistic is that? The underlying assumption is that any other forces potentially driving the exchange rate – such as political factors, institutions, and capital flows – do not play a role. The prevailing current account and exchange rate between the USA and China are but one example where this is clearly not the case. Our closure rules (discussed in the next section) allow for a more complete analysis.

Labour markets

There is no space whatsoever for unemployment in the version of the Bank's model described in the quotation above from van der Mensbrugghe, which implies the potential outcomes of trade liberalisation do not include lack of jobs or under-utilisation of capital. Bank models can address issues of employment (or shifts in the trade balance) but usually its modelling department *chooses* not to do so.[36]

Unlike the World Bank, we report and compare simulation results with and without an assumption of full employment. Not only employment, but also the current account and the government balance are important indicators of macro-economic performance. The World Bank freezes these three major variables out of the analysis and focuses almost exclusively on welfare measures. More realistically, which of these variables is (or are) endogenous and which exogenous depends on the specific closure assumptions made by the modeller.

Other differences

A few more details should be mentioned: in our model, all of the government's expenditure is assumed to go to the services sector. Investment demand is only for industrial goods. Intermediate imports are assumed to be exclusively intra-regional in the developed world, but exclusively extra-regional in SSA. The data appear to allow for such a simplification as, first, the overwhelming majority of imports to SSA come from outside the region and, second, it is likely that intermediates such as industrial goods and machinery have to be imported from the Northern hemisphere.

Closure assumptions

As mentioned above, and in contrast to the World Bank, we apply different closure rules.[37] Economic theory implies causation in the sense that one variable in a formal model drives another (very often 'dual' to the first). In the labour market context discussed above, causation runs either from employment to wages or from wages to employment. If employment is given – or 'full' – then the wage follows from the functional relationship between the two, or vice versa. Thus, the modeller has to make an *a priori* decision about which variable is endogenous to the model. If, as in the World Bank model, employment, the current account, and the government deficit are exogenous and remain unchanged, the model will generate changes in wages, exchange rates, and taxes but will not be able to provide policy recommendations about rather important *quantity* macro variables.

On the other hand, in certain situations it is perfectly reasonable to assume, for example, a fixed current account. If a model addresses the short run and focuses on, say, Germany – a country with a persistent and relatively stable trade surplus – the current account might not be the major concern of the policies in question. However, many countries subject to the Doha negotiations are prone to high current account deficits; in fact, high deficits are characteristic of recent financial crises in developing countries. To put it carefully, there is no reason not to consider possible effects of liberalisation on the current account.

It is unnecessary to claim that *any* closure assumption reflects the 'true' direction of causation. Applied economists are well aware that certain models and their assumptions fit certain situations, periods, and countries and might not add insight in other circumstances. For a model on a global scale and an issue as hotly debated as the Doha Round it simply seems prudent to look at the issues from different perspectives. Suppose empirical research could show (or have shown) that the exchange rate is a highly flexible international price that adjusts to guarantee balanced trade with 50 per cent probability. Should policy analysis not address the other 50 per cent as well?

Thus, we will outline a few selected scenarios and subsequently discuss our simulation results, with the aim of highlighting the limitations of the World Bank's modelling strategy, as well as shedding light on the current negotiations at the WTO.

At the macro-economic level in either region, three key flows of funds balances have to be satisfied and two factor markets have to be described, which gives 32 different closure combinations between the private balance (savings and investment), the public balance (government spending and revenue), the foreign balance (current account and the exchange rate), and the factor markets (capital, labour, and profit and wage rate, respectively). We will limit ourselves to two exemplary closures: the *Bank's closure* and an *absorption closure*.

The 'World Bank' closure

The macro-economics of various closure rules has been discussed in Part I. Here we briefly review the key elements (see Figure 4 for an overview). The Bank's closure works along the lines of the elasticities approach to the balance of payments (as extended by the fiscal effects discussed in Part I and illustrated below). The government deficit, the current account, and employment levels are exogenous. Simulation results under these assumptions do not allow one to draw conclusions about the likely future behaviour of these variables. They are set in stone at their base-year levels, so that any changes – however drastic – affect neither the public and foreign deficits nor the (un)employment rate. Consistent with neoclassical theory, adjustment is mainly carried out by variation of prices. As will be seen, however, the price changes often dance to macro-economic and not micro-economic tunes.

In common with goods prices, factor prices (wage and profit rate) and the exchange rate shift so that the aforementioned constraints are satisfied. If the government deficit is predetermined, the government is not able to finance expenditure by increased borrowing. Tariff and subsidy rates are simulation parameters and prices adjust endogenously; hence the only variable that can adjust in the government balance is the household consumption tax.[38] In the private balance, investment adjusts to savings and, lastly, the exchange rate adjusts so that the current account stays constant. As emphasised in Part I, the exchange rate in our set-up is a variable that appears explicitly instead of being a metaphor.

With regard to factor markets, full employment rules. In the Bank's closure, the totals of employed labour and capital in the two economies are assumed to be constant. At the sectoral level, however, labour–capital ratios can (and must) shift in any new solution.

Figure 4: Closure rules of the two models

	Bank's closure (LINKAGE)	Absorption closure
Private balance: investment & saving	**Neoclassical investment**: investment adjusts to savings, a function of income and a set of parameters. *Investment is savings-driven, following the standard neoclassical presumption that any funds available are channelled into productive investment.*	**Keynesian investment**: investment is exogenous (constant). *Investment is decided upon by the 'entrepreneur', and, following Keynesian theory, generates the savings necessary to finance itself from increased income.*
Public balance: government deficit & tax revenue	The deficit is constant, and taxes adjust to guarantee that. *There is neither an economic theory nor actual country experience that supports this kind of adjustment. Governments cannot spontaneously increase taxes to balance the budget; that is why current Doha negotiations deal with adjustment funds for developing countries which rely heavily on tariff revenue to finance expenditure.*	Lump-sum taxes are proportional to income, and the government deficit adjusts to balance the difference between public expenditures and revenue. *Governments across the globe use automatic stabilisers and public works programmes to counter negative effects of economic downturns – meaning the deficit (and not tax revenue) is endogenous*
Foreign balance: exchange rate & current account	**Elasticities adjustment to the balance of payments**: The exchange rate adjusts to hold the current account constant. *A constant current account corresponds to the idea of balanced trade: an exchange rate change combined with the 'right' elasticities ensures that an increase in the value of imports is met by an equivalent increase in the value of exports.*	**Income or absorption adjustment to the balance of payments**: The current account adjusts according to demand shifts, and the exchange rate is exogenous. *Given the constant exchange rate and the elasticities, trade flows and consequently income accommodate the price changes due to liberalisation.*
Labour markets: employment & wages	**Neoclassical labour market**: Employment is constant, and the wage endogenous. *Wages adjust to a given (fixed, or full) level of employment, which corresponds to the neoclassical conviction that if only wages are flexible enough, everybody will find work.*	**'Keynesian' labour market**: The wage is constant, and employment endogenous. *If the wage is rigid due to institutional arrangements (e.g. unions), or represents a subsistence wage, unemployment is possible, as firms might not hire all labour supplied at this wage.*

'Absorption' closure

Our absorption closure presents the natural antithesis to the Bank's closure. In all macro-economic balances, causality assumptions are reversed.

Taxes on households are held to be simply proportional to value added, so that the government deficit adjusts to finance expenditure and absorb the revenue reduction when tariffs are cut. Government borrowing moves up and down in any functioning economy, even when it is hypothetically constrained by IMF conditionalities or Maastricht accords. Letting it play its proper role in a model simulation is simple common sense.

Fixing the exchange rate leaves the current account as an adjusting variable. It permits macro-economic 'absorption' of shifting import and export *quantities*, instead of an 'elastic' adjustment of trade flows to international *prices*.

In the private balance, investment is predetermined. This view follows Keynesian theory in which entrepreneurs decide about the investment projects according to long-term expectations and *animal spirits* rather than automatically channelling available savings flows into physical investment.

Lastly, in this exercise we abandon the assumption of full employment. Employment levels of both capital and labour are variable, and wage and profit rates are fixed. As in the Bank's closure, workers and capital can freely move from sector to sector, but may end up under- or over-employed. Demand changes *can* have an impact on employment.

The implications of the different closures are summarised in Figure 5. The limitations of the Bank's closure become immediately obvious: simulations run under this model simply do not consider the most important quantity-related macro-economic indicators, besides real GDP.

Figure 5: What the different closure rules imply: which macroeconomic indicators are analysed?

	Bank's closure (LINKAGE)	Absorption closure
GDP	Yes	Yes
'Welfare'	Yes	Yes
Government deficit	No	Yes
Exchange rate	Our 'replica': Yes. LINKAGE: No, the model does not feature an explicit exchange rate.	No
Current account	No	Yes
Employment	No	Yes
Wages	Yes	No

Results

In this section we present the results of these different simulations. A key result is that the causality assumptions determine simulation results. Thus, endogenising the government deficit produces completely different results from when it is left constant.

Simulation strategies

The World Bank usually contrasts a model's results under complete liberalisation with some 'likely' Doha scenario which would take into account political realities, the current state of the negotiations, and the principles underlying them. The developing world would presumably allow more non-agricultural market access for exporters from the North, and the developed world would lower agricultural protection by removing subsidies for agro-exporters as well as tariffs on imports. In this scenario, given the development emphasis of the Doha round and various 'special treatment' clauses, SSA would be required to cut tariffs by less then ROW would. Overall, tariffs and subsidies would be reduced but not eliminated.[39]

Limiting the analysis to 'only' three liberalisation scenarios, two closure rules and, say, three different regimes of trade elasticities already gives a wide range of combinations to discuss. The difference between our modelling strategy and that of the World Bank becomes obvious. Instead of including scores of regions and sectors we attempt to describe broad patterns of results from different theoretical perspectives. Certainly, estimating regional and sectoral changes in detail is invaluable for policy makers, but given the task at hand it seems unlikely that additional insights could be gained from greater disaggregation. Our simulation strategy is summarised in Figure 6.

Figure 6: Simulation strategy

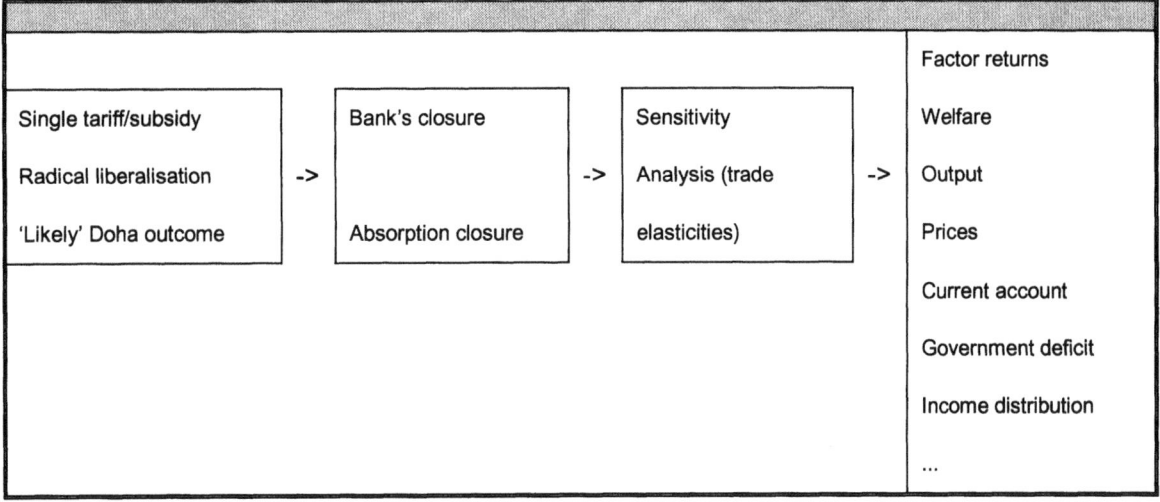

Sensitivity analysis

Sensitivity analysis is an important dimension of a complete model description. CGE models are fed a banquet of parameters that at best come from econometric analysis, but often from prior belief and (more or less) educated judgements on the part of the modeller. It is indispensable to investigate the effects of changes of parameters on results and the model's policy recommendations. Parameter values derived from a mixture of econometrics – itself often not to be trusted – and a modeller's considered opinions could quickly render conclusions irrelevant if they were not robust in the face of 'reasonable' changes.

The most important – and controversial – parameters in LINKAGE/GTAP-style trade models are the Armington elasticities. As discussed in Part I, the World Bank has been criticised for using elasticity values that are 'too high'. Higher elasticities improve the responsiveness of trade flows to price changes, and this in turn requires less adjustment in other macro-economic variables. We will focus on Armington elasticity values.[40]

SSA agricultural tariff elimination (Bank's closure)

The baseline configuration features trade elasticities of a lower average magnitude and with stronger econometric support than the ones commonly used in LINKAGE or GTAP. Completely removing, in a first exercise, the external agricultural tariff in the developing region – i.e. the tariff that SSA applies to agricultural imports from ROW – and applying the Bank's closure rules has small, *negative* effects on welfare in SSA.

That the effects are small is not surprising in light of the fact that SSA's GDP is around 1.1 per cent of ROW's (see the discussion of the SAM in Appendix 1). A change in just one tariff in a small open economy has effects on that economy, but triggers close to zero response in the larger partner.[41]

In any scenario, prices and quantities must be considered separately. Given the functional relationships among tariffs, prices, and wage and profit rates, we can trace a chain of causation in the results: a tariff decrease lowers the agricultural sector supply price Z in the Armington cost function and the output price P in the cost decomposition of domestic output in SSA. Real value-added V decreases slightly and factor returns fall, which in turn pull the value-added price Q and the overall price level down.[42]

Why does real value-added decline? Looking at V takes us to quantity variables. The change in relative prices due to the tariff decrease increases SSA demand for agricultural imports. In this particular simulation, real imports rise by more than 14 per cent, whereas the average change in trade flows hovers at about 1 per cent.[43] As an illustration, say consumer households substitute Iowa-grown maize for the local product in their mealy-meal, so that domestic agriculture faces an adverse shift in demand. Real output in SSA agriculture declines by about one percentage point,[44] because the adverse demand shock is *not* neutralised by a positive shift in export demand. As we will see in other simulations, this problem disappears with higher trade elasticities. In the present case, relative price changes induce demand shifts that translate into negative GDP growth.

The contraction of value added is a consequence of the core fiscal adjustment (noted repeatedly above) in the Bank's closure. The SSA government is constrained to borrow constant amounts from the private sector and from ROW but receives less tariff revenue due to liberalisation. Its only possible recourse in a LINKAGE world is to raise taxes on household income to balance its flow of funds. Raising taxes crowds out private consumption, which provides the basis for the little triangle welfare calculations commonly applied. Two effects contribute to a decrease in welfare: the decline in value added tightens the private sector budget constraint and consequently diminished consumption levels are further stifled by increased taxes. The welfare losses are small – a third of a percentage point – and other macro-economic performance indicators (employment, current account, fiscal deficit) are constant by assumption.

SSA industrial tariff elimination (absorption closure)

Tracing through a similar exercise illustrates how adjustment works in the absorption closure. This time we look at the effects of removing SSA's tariff on industrial imports. Again, trade elasticities are assumed to be 'normal'.

Macro causality now runs along Keynesian lines, with quantities instead of prices bearing the weight of adjustment. The wage, profit, and exchange rates are fixed and the current account and government deficit are endogenous. As before, we analyse price and quantity changes. The former are essentially the same – as was to be expected since we did not change the model *structure*. The industrial supply price Z decreases in response to the tariff removal. Factor prices are exogenous, so that the price of value-added Q cannot change. The difference from the previous scenario is that domestic output is not forced to contract if the export response lacks strength. In fact, because the foreign deficit is free to rise, neither exports nor GDP need move to balance an import surge.

The simulation results are clear: the current account worsens tremendously with rising imports, resulting from the shift in the relative prices of domestic and foreign manufactures. In order to satisfy its flow of funds constraint and match the loss in tariff revenue, the government (now free to borrow more from the private sector while holding income taxes constant) increases its deficit spending.

Manufactures from the developed world are important inputs into the SSA economy. The fall in input costs therefore increases output, at least in the agricultural and service sectors. Demand for manufactures themselves shifts towards foreign products, and real domestic output in the industrial sector contracts. Still, the overall effects on economic activity are positive. Because the government does not raise taxes, real output and value-added growth lead to an increase in consumption. SSA enjoys welfare increases, here about 1.3 per cent of GDP. Employment is proportional to value added, so that expansion in this exercise leads to higher demand for labour and the utilisation of capital.

Sadly, the picture is not as rosy as might appear.[45] Little triangle measures of welfare gains, derived from 'first principles',[46] have the advantage of being widely accepted and comparable (under the rather stringent assumptions of Utopian capitalism), but really only make sense if other macro-economic indicators are held constant by assumption. Looking at the jumps in both foreign and public deficits,[47] the risks faced by this developing economy can be identified. Chronic indebtedness, debt crises, capital flight, and political instability are only some of the problems it would confront in the not-too distant future.

Fiscal implications of output subsidy and import tariff elimination

We are almost ready to discuss simulations of full liberalisation, in which all tariffs and output and export subsidies are removed. In the World Bank's model, this implies that any distortion (as shown in Figure 2) is eliminated, and all those roughly 5,000 little triangles are freed to enlarge global welfare. In our model, the export subsidy on manufacturing exports, the output subsidies in all three sectors, and the tariffs on the two traded goods are reduced to zero. Let's start by looking at results in the Bank's closure.[48]

Total employment, the current account, and the government deficit remain, of course, unchanged. Before getting into the details of complete liberalisation it is helpful to disentangle the effects of full output subsidy removal on the one hand, and full tariff removal on the other. Fiscal effects again dominate the scene.

The output subsidy makes up a large part of the total expenditures of the government, and saving those costs translates into lower taxes on households because the fiscal deficit and government consumption are fixed. All things being equal, lower taxes increase disposable income and thereby consumption, which leads to potentially hefty increases in welfare.[49] Tariff liberalisation, on the contrary, decreases fiscal revenue instead of expenditure and forces the government to raise taxes, which crowds out consumption and reduces welfare. These are *macro* effects. Nevertheless, they go a long way toward determining the characteristics of the Bank's micro-economically oriented closure.

Evidently, the welfare consequences of full liberalisation in the Bank's closure depend not only on trade elasticities, but also on the initial height of tariffs (for government revenue) and subsidies (for government expenditures). Generously interpreted, the welfare result following subsidy removal could be seen as an efficiency gain, in the sense that producers employ resources in the most productive way possible, instead of being misled by 'wrong' price signals from the subsidies.

Less generously, and probably more realistically, one could interpret the welfare increase as the model's inability to capture the socio-economic adjustment costs that come with such a policy change. US and European trade negotiators do not block major modifications to their agricultural protection schemes because they disdain textbook economic efficiency. Rather, it is because a few million farmers in Europe and thousands of agribusiness enterprises in the USA would fail if their subsidies were slashed. Extreme and politically damaging jumps in food prices could easily ensue, and the erstwhile farmers and their employees would not smoothly metamorphose into software programmers. World Bank analysts apparently deem such metamorphoses possible. The equivalent assumption about businesses would probably be that owners have hedged any potential losses.

To summarise, full output subsidy removal in the Bank's closure has strongly positive welfare effects, for the reasons discussed above. 'Money' freed from the government's intervening, visible hand stimulates demand and real output increases. Import growth is strong, but high exports balance the current account due to a robust devaluation of the SSA currency. Prices *increase* in SSA, but (along with factor returns) *decrease* in ROW.

Radical tariff elimination, on the other hand, triggers only small price changes. Composite supply increases due to the growth in trade, but domestic output decreases across the board. As import prices fall, demand for foreign product rises relative to domestic product; the consumption crunch following the rise in taxes consequently depresses domestic real output.

Full liberalisation with the Bank's closure

Having sorted these things out, we can return to the initial question: what effects does full liberalisation have in the Bank's closure? The leftmost bars in Figure 7 show the welfare results with reasonable elasticities in both SSA and ROW, while the broken line indicates the average Armington elasticity. SSA loses slightly more than half a percentage point[50] of GDP, ROW gains *around* three per cent. If our base-year data had featured higher subsidy and lower tariff rates, SSA could very well have shown higher – i.e. positive – welfare gains. ROW's welfare gains are due to the fact that subsidies were high.

Figure 7: Welfare changes relative to GDP: full liberalisation in the Bank's closure with different Armington elasticities

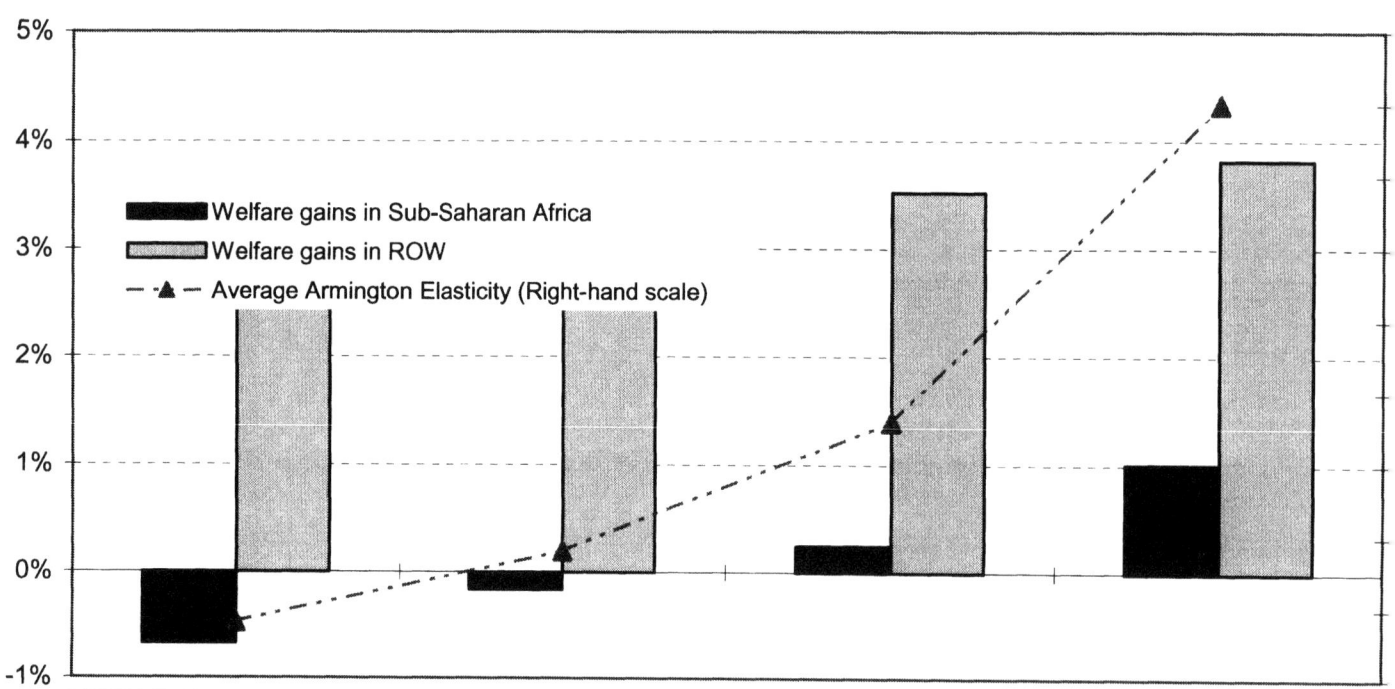

Figure 7: The percentage change in welfare is the ratio of the absolute welfare change to GDP. The (standard) welfare measure used is the average of Equivalent and Compensating Variation, which compare pre- and post-liberalisation utility either at pre- or post-liberalisation prices. It is immediately obvious that the welfare outcome, at least for the smaller, poorer region, depends crucially on the size of the elasticities. The first pair of bars from the left show the results of a simulation with trade elasticities that have stronger empirical support than those to the right.

Full liberalisation under the absorption closure

Let's look at liberalisation under the absorption closure, with results for sub-Saharan Africa summarised in Figure 8. As above, it helps to analyse subsidy and tariff liberalisation separately. Removing all subsidies in this rather Keynesian economy has interesting effects. Subsidy elimination triggers a heavy contraction of demand as the government saves the funds it previously spent on subsidies to reduce its deficit. Taxes are not endogenous to close the government's accounts as in the Bank's closure. With government spending on services fixed, and negative public savings decreasing in magnitude (subsidies no longer need to be financed), government income increases, with double-digit growth rates in both regions. Using the same expression as before, the 'money' freed up from subsidies is transferred to lower public debt instead of to consumers in the form of lower taxes. Thus, subsidy removal suppresses demand and, with falling demand, imports as well as exports decrease. Consequently, unemployment rises and welfare decreases.

On the positive side, the foreign deficit is relatively stable and the public deficit is cut in half in SSA and almost eliminated in the developed world. Where would such an economy be headed? IMF adjustment programmes often prescribe contractionary policies to induce trust and increase inflows of foreign capital. In the best case, this might happen; in the worst case, unemployment and income losses may spur political unrest and severely impede development.

Figure 8: Selected indicators for SSA macro performance relative to GDP

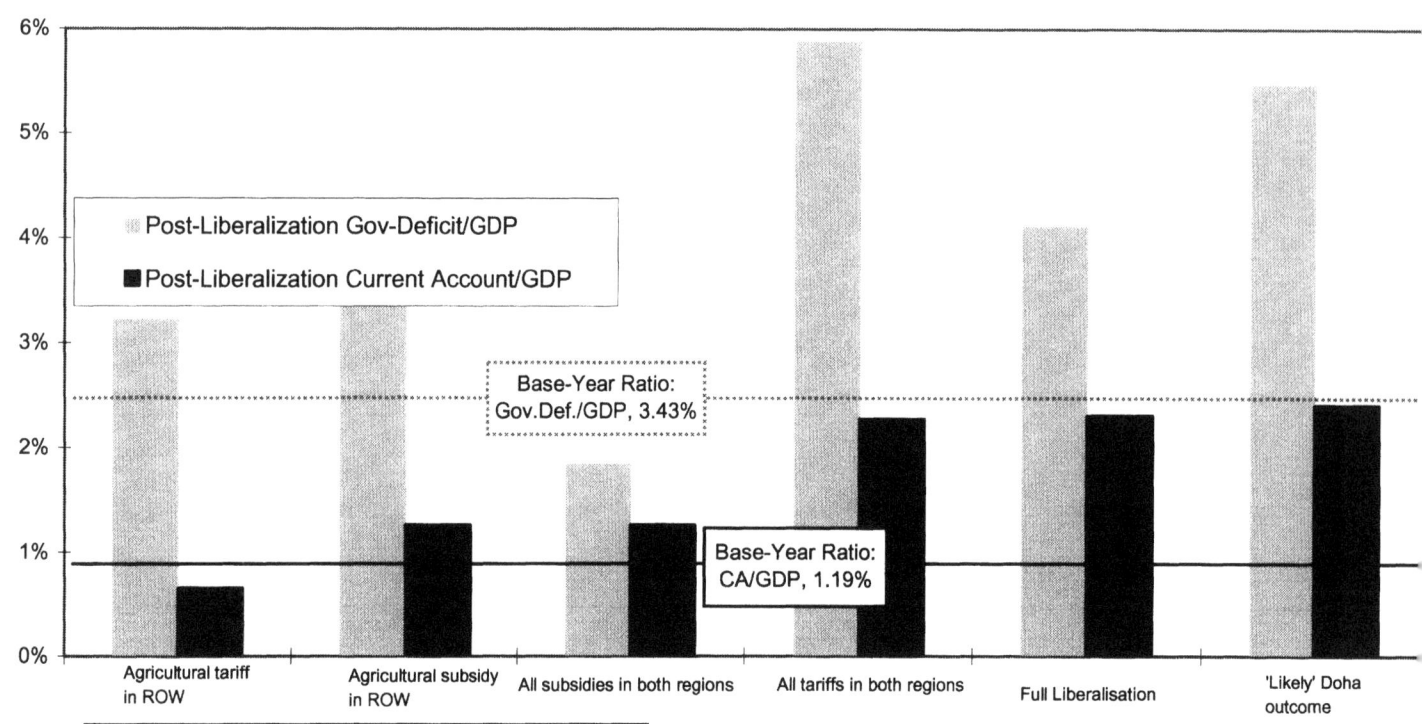

Figure 8: The bars show the ratio of the given indicator to GDP, post-liberalisation. Each pair of bars corresponds to a specific liberalisation scenario and should be compared with the base-year levels of the respective ratio. The three leftmost scenarios show an improvement or an (almost) unchanged current account. The government defiict improves in two. The three rightmost scenarios show deterioration in both indicators.

Radical tariff reform has opposite results. The current account and public deficits deteriorate, but employment, output, and welfare improve. The key to understanding these results is the same as in other closures and liberalisation scenarios; it is the interaction between government revenue and deficit on the one side and the various demand responses (consumption, imports, and exports) on the other. Here, the government loses a source of revenue – tariffs – but still has to finance subsidies and other expenditures. With the deficit as the adjusting variable, taxes do *not* increase and so do not crowd out consumption. Moreover, lower import prices increase demand for foreign products and reduce costs for inputs; consequently trade and domestic production expand. Value added rises with output, and employment, consumption, and welfare all follow.

However, if the willingness or ability to substitute imports for domestic product is moderate, the export response of an economically small region like SSA cannot be strong enough to counteract the import surge from ROW. Thus, the current account deficit increases.

Combined, liberalisation of tariffs and subsidies brings about the worst of both, at least for the developing region: rises in foreign and public deficits, and falls in consumption, output, and employment. The benefits from lower import prices are too low relative to the contraction due to subsidy removal but, on the other hand, the deficit-lowering effects of the latter are not high enough to improve the public balances. As subsidies play a more important role in ROW, the deficit decreases. Still, global real output diminishes.

A 'likely' Doha outcome

In a 'likely' Doha outcome, we see the same principles at work as in the examples discussed so far. Our Doha scenario takes into account the state of the negotiations after Hong Kong. Firstly, developed country export subsidies will be phased out. Secondly, we reflect the major concerns of the negotiating blocks: developing countries demand 'real'[51] decreases in domestic producer support in ROW, while developed countries ask for improvements in non-agricultural market access in SSA. Therefore, our likely Doha outcome features a full removal of export subsidies and elimination of agricultural output subsidies in ROW and industrial tariffs in SSA. The extent of this liberalisation is certainly stylised, but it gives us a blueprint from which to discuss the interests of the involved parties.

Based on 'normal' elasticities, Figure 9 summarises the simulation results for Bank and absorption closures in both regions. The lower part of the diagram shows changes in selected indicators for SSA, some of which are constant in the Bank's closure. The upper part shows changes in ROW's macro performance, leaving aside the current account, as that is simply the negative of SSA's. We observe the relatively high volatility in the 'Keynesian' simulations, with risks especially for Africa, but also slight employment losses in the developed world.

Let us begin our analysis again with the Bank's closure, where deficits and employment are fixed. Lowering the agricultural subsidy reduces fiscal outlays, which get transferred to consumers through lower taxes. Hence, ROW's consumers experience an increase in income and gains in welfare. In SSA, the lower tariff rate decreases import prices for manufactures, which boosts imports in that sector and thereby increases total supply. The export response is tame, because ROW did not further improve its non-agricultural market access, so that domestic output decreases in the industrial sector. However, the fall in output in the agricultural sector abroad leads to an increase in export demand for agricultural products. The drop in tariff revenue, moreover, is not steep enough to strangle consumption completely: despite a fall in nominal consumption spending, welfare rises.[52]

As seen before, simulations under the absorption assumptions have opposite results: tariff removal is beneficial, as the increase in the deficit allows consumers to go on a spending spree, whereas subsidy removal has negative effects on output, employment, and welfare because of the contractionary policy of the government. Consequently, our likely Doha scenario produces moderate welfare gains in SSA and small losses in the developed world.[53]

It is important to realise how very sensitive all these simulation results are not only to the specific liberalisation scenario and the base-year data set, but moreover to the assumptions made about which economic agents change their behaviour, and in what regard, post-reform.

Figure 9: Selected indicators under different closures – 'likely' Doha outcome

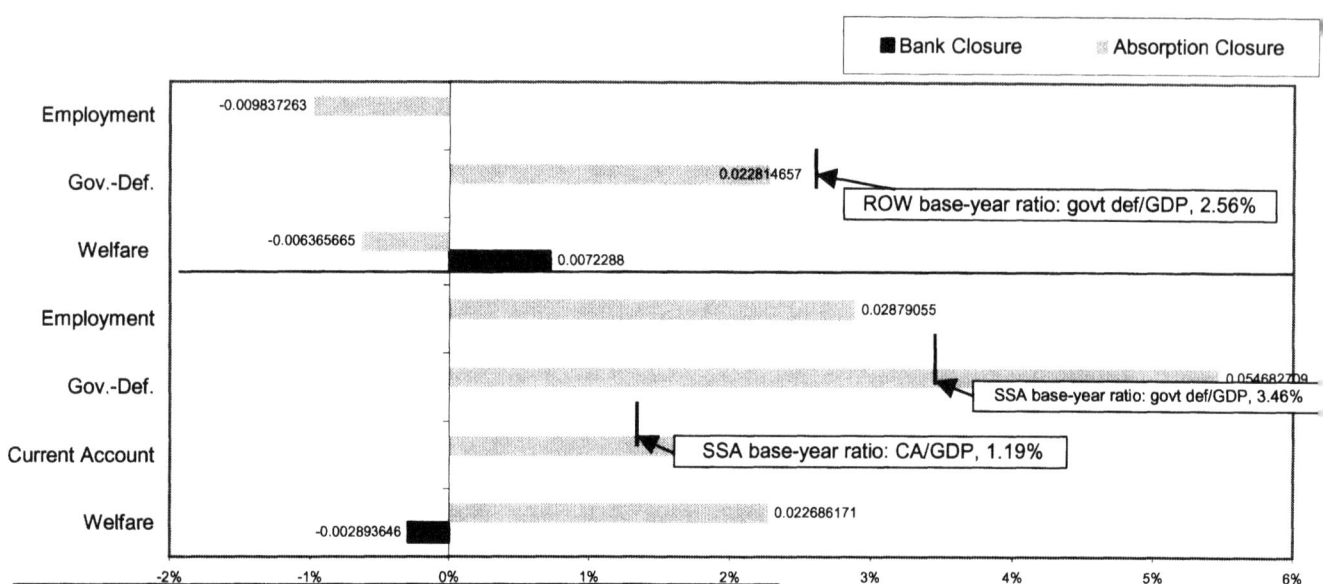

Figure 9: The upper part of the figure shows changes in the rest of the world and the lower part shows sub-Saharan Africa. Employment changes are relative to the base-year level, whereas government deficit, current account, and welfare are relative to GDP. The current account for ROW is the reverse of SSA, so it is sufficient to show it once. All changes are simulation results of a 'likely' Doha scenario. The grey bars indicate results under our absorption closure, the black ones the Bank's closure. The figure demonstrates how the Bank's closure suppresses key macro indicators, and that these potentially worsen, once taken into account.

Unsurprisingly, the Bank's closure shows results where macro-economic performance is overall more stable (see Figure 9). Unsurprising, because most indicators to which policy makers pay attention are held constant. Still, welfare depends on the specific simulation scenarios, and it is in fact rather straightforward to see negative welfare changes due to a crowding out of consumption.

Equally unsurprisingly, the Keynesian closure shows relatively volatile macro behaviour. Employment, output, current account, and public deficit changes have strong spillover effects on economic activity. The multiplier effect from a higher government deficit and income gains from import adjustments have positive welfare effects but, as discussed above, they pose great risks for an increasingly vulnerable economy. Figure 9 shows the high volatility in selected key indicators of sub-Saharan Africa.

Armington elasticities matter

Lastly, we should note how crucial the size of the Armington trade elasticities is for all these effects. The simulations discussed thus far have all been based on 'normal' elasticities, meaning that they average around 1.5 – a reasonable mid-point of a range supported by empirical research. It is obvious that a policy conclusion to the effect that 'SSA should not liberalise because simulations show a negative welfare change of a third of a percentage point' is meaningless because such a small change could be bigger in magnitude and/or have a different sign depending on the complex interaction of all parameters, base-year data, and functional and closure-related assumptions. However, Figure 7 clearly shows the positive relationship in such a model between the magnitude of Armington elasticities and welfare effects in the small, dependent region.

Conclusions

We finish with two sets of conclusions, one with regard to our critique of CGE (and especially World Bank) modelling of trade liberalisation and the other concerning current WTO liberalisation negotiations.

First, the Armington trade specification that lies at the heart of Bank models is riddled with problems.

Its fundamental weakness is the 'fiscal adjustment effect' described in detail in Part I. Instead of having a neutral impact on aggregate demand, a tariff reduction and the offsetting direct tax increase built into the LINKAGE specification lead to demand contraction. The *direct* impact of the higher tax on reducing real consumer spending is greater than the *indirect* effect of tariff reduction on cutting its cost, because there are non-import cost components in the Armington aggregate supply price and the price applies to more components of demand than just consumption.

The effects of subsidy removal go in the opposite direction. With roughly 5,000 separate commodity markets in a full LINKAGE simulation and associated tariffs and subsidies interacting in an extremely complicated fashion, the implication is that the World Bank's estimates of its preferred indicators of 'welfare gains' from liberalisation are subject to biases of unknown and potentially large magnitude and direction. Furthermore, Armington over-emphasises the potential benefits of liberalisation by granting national economies monopoly power, and this sort of product differentiation is an inappropriate description of trade at the commodity level (which often takes the form of intra-company trade by multinational corporations). In sum, although the Armington specification is convenient for modelling purposes, its empirical and theoretical defects render it almost useless in practical terms.

Second, the magnitude of the trade elasticities chosen for a model greatly affects its simulation results. The higher the elasticities, the stronger the substitution effect between imports and domestic products, leading to enhanced welfare gains and reduction of adverse shifts in the terms of trade. In the relevant World Bank publications, elasticities are usually set at levels higher than those supported by econometric evidence.

Third, LINKAGE muddles micro-economics and trade theory on the one hand with open-economy macro-economics on the other. Consistent with the former, the Bank model goes a long way toward describing a 'general equilibrium' with plenty of markets. Inconsistent with the latter, LINKAGE hides national exchange rates – the key macro-level prices – behind all the varying commodity prices and hundreds of factor prices. This level of disaggregation and detail does little to clarify the issues under debate and causes a lot of confusion about what the model is actually doing. The confusion is not alleviated by the extremely complicated Gothic architecture of the Bank's model.

Fourth, despite its 'absence' in the World Bank model, the exchange rate adjusts to balance international trade. The idea is firmly rooted in Ricardo's theory of comparative advantage, which says that *if* the exchange rate responds only to trade flows and in that sense presents a pure 'specie flow,' trade, on average, will be balanced, as each country specialises in the sector featuring the relatively higher productivity. In the real world, however, there are plenty of reasons why such an adjustment might not take place, and why trade might not be balanced. Interventions (such as from the Chinese and Japanese central banks in US dollar markets nowadays) are only one example; political risks and conflicts as well as capital movements are others. As capital movements *by far* overshadow trade flows, the exchange rate is likely not 'free' to adjust to changes in trade.

Fifth, the choice of causality assumptions built into LINKAGE ('closure' in the jargon) is of critical relevance to simulation results. It is outright negligent to assume that the most central macro-economic indicators do not change in response to any liberalisation scenario. Especially in developing countries (with historically large trade deficits, huge debt problems, and a large informal economy with under-employment in modern sectors), fixing the current account, the government deficit, and employment makes no sense. Neither an economics degree nor modelling capacity are necessary to see that risks from trade liberalisation appear diminished if the candidate 'risky' variables are held constant. An honest simulation strategy should include various closure regimes, so that policy makers can assess different situations. As it is unlikely that there will be a consensus about the direction of causalities in the global economy any time soon, policy makers should be able to base their decisions – given their mandate – on a set of possible scenarios instead of the 'World Bank version'. This is especially true in developing countries, where technical capacities and modelling expertise are often limited, which means that governments must depend on Bank advice.

Finally, even if they were estimated correctly by LINKAGE, the model's 'little triangle' measures of welfare gains presuppose that the economy is always at full employment and that economic agents worldwide are basically uniform in tastes, access to resources, and income levels. Such a state of 'Utopian capitalism' simply does not exist. Nor is it clear, under the state of capitalism that really exists, that international trade negotiators really know what the measures are trying to indicate. In practical policymaking, they are far more likely to pay attention to the macro-economic indicators that Bank models suppress.

What insight does the World Bank model add to the controversy surrounding the Doha Development Agenda? Due to the sheer size of LINKAGE and similar models, we may be able to learn about distributive issues: which of the many sectors in which of the many countries win, and which ones lose? Insisting on what we called above the Bank's 'closure', however, limits the relevance of LINKAGE's simulation results, because policy recommendations require a preamble spelling out the model's unrealistic assumptions about the current account, the government deficit, and the employment of labour and capital.

Our model, although it incorporates a great deal of LINKAGE's unrealism, shows that:

- If trade elasticities are lower than the Bank stipulates, sub-Saharan Africa faces welfare losses even in an otherwise most optimistic situation which rules out all macro-economic shocks.

- If the current account is allowed to respond to trade liberalisation, and imports to one region grow stronger than that region's exports, it is Africa – and not the developed world – that faces a deteriorating trade balance.

- If the analysis includes the government deficit, the African public balance often deteriorates, whereas the rest of the world's fiscal position improves.

- If employment and income are variable, they might very well increase in sub-Saharan Africa, but do so in tandem with mounting trade deficits and foreign debt, which renders these advances temporary.

Our final conclusion has to be that developing countries would be ill-advised to follow the radical recommendations of the World Bank's liberalisation strategy insofar as it rests on results from the LINKAGE model.

References

Ackerman, F. (2005) 'The Shrinking Gains from Trade: A Critical Assessment of Doha Round Projections', Global Development and Environment Institute (Tufts University) Working Paper.

Anderson, K. and W. Martin (2005) 'Agricultural Trade Reform and the Doha Development Agenda', World Bank Policy Research Working Paper 3607.

____ (2005) 'Agricultural Market Access: The Key to Doha Success', World Bank Trade Note 23.

Anderson, K., W. Martin, and D. van der Mensbrugghe (2005) 'Would Multilateral Trade Reform Benefit Sub-Saharan Africa?' World Bank Policy Research Working Paper 3616.

Armington, P. S. (1969) 'A Theory of Demand for Products Distinguished by Place of Production', International Monetary Fund Staff Papers 16.

Arrow, K. J. and F. H. Hahn (1971) *General Competitive Analysis*, New York: North-Holland.

Cline, W. R. (2004) *Trade Policy and Global Poverty*, Washington DC: Institute for International Economics.

Dimaran, B. V., R. A. McDougall and T. W. Hertel (2002) 'Behavioral parameters', in B. V. Dimaran and R. A. McDougall, *Global Trade, Assistance, and Production: The Gtap 5 Data Base*, Purdue University: Center for Global Trade Analysis.

Dupuit, J. (1844) 'De la Mesure de l'Utilité des Travaux Publics,' *Annales de Ponts et Chaussées* 8: pp332–75.

FAO (2005) 'Trade Policy Simulation Models: Estimating Global Impacts of Agricultural Trade Policy Reform in the Doha Round', Rome: FAO Trade Policy Technical Notes on Issues Related to the WTO Negotiations on Agriculture.

Godley, W. (1996) 'A Simple Model of the Whole World with Free Trade, Free Capital Movements, and Floating Exchange Rates', Annandale-on-Hudson New York: Jerome Levy Economics Institute.

GTAP (2005) 'GTAP 6 Database', West Lafayette Indiana: Center for Global Trade Analysis.

Harberger, A. C. (1959) 'Using the Resources at Hand More Efficiently', American Economic Association (Papers and Proceedings), 49(2): pp134–46.

HM Treasury, Department of Trade and Industry (2004) 'Estimations of global welfare gains from trade liberalisation', in *Trade and the Global Economy: The Role of International Trade in Productivity, Economic Reform and Growth*, Norwich: HM Treasury.

Johansen, L. (1960) *A Multi-Sectoral Study of Economic Growth*, Amsterdam: North-Holland.

Keynes, J. M. (1936) *The General Theory of Employment, Interest, and Money*, New York: Harcourt, Brace & World.

Kirman, A. P. (1992) 'Whom or what does the representative agent represent?', *Journal of Economic Perspectives* 6: pp117–36.

Kraev, E. (2005) *Estimating GDP Effects of Trade Liberalization on Developing Countries*, London: Christian Aid.

Leontief, W. (1986) *Input-Output Economics*, New York: Oxford University Press.

Little, I. M. D. (1957) *A Critique of Welfare Economics*, Oxford: Oxford University Press.

Oxfam (2005) 'US Farm Subsidies Offer "Smoke and Mirrors"', Oxfam International press release.

____ (2005) 'No Real Gains for Poor in EU Trade Offer', Oxfam International press release.

Sagoff, M. (1988) *The Economy of the Earth: Philosophy, Law and the Environment*, Cambridge, New York and Melbourne: Cambridge University Press.

Samuelson, P. (2004) 'Where Ricardo and Mill rebut and confirm arguments of mainstream economics supporting globalization', *Journal of Economic Perspectives* 18: pp135–46.

Stanford, J. O. (1992) 'C.G.E. Models of North American Free Trade: A Critique of Methods and Assumptions', Testimony to the United States International Trade Commission.

Stone, J. R. N. (1966) 'The social accounts from a consumer point of view', *Review of Income and Wealth* 12(1): pp1–33.

Taylor, L. and S. L. Black (1974) 'Practical general equilibrium estimation of resource pulls under trade liberalization', *Journal of International Economics* 4(1): pp37–58.

Taylor, L. and F. J. Lysy (1979) 'Vanishing income redistributions: Keynesian clues about model surprises in the short run', *Journal of Development Economics* 6: pp11–29.

Taylor, L. (2004) *Reconstructing Macroeconomics: Structuralist Proposals and Critiques of the Mainstream*, Cambridge, Massachusetts: Harvard University Press.

van der Mensbrugghe, D. (2005) 'Linkage technical reference document', Development Prospects Group, The World Bank.

Varian, H. R. (1992) *Microeconomic Analysis*, New York: W. W. Norton & Company.

Appendix 1: Illustrative SSA/ROW Data

In this appendix we illustrate how the data used in trade models are organised in a social accounting matrix (or SAM), which also serves as an introduction to their macro-economics. The figure on the next page presents a SAM we put together for SSA and ROW using numbers from the extensive GTAP database (for more details see Part II). Data manipulation was involved (in part due to deficiencies in the sources) but the matrix is perhaps at least representative of the regions' production and trade patterns early in the present decade. Numbers for two sectors are presented – agriculture and the rest of the economy (or 'industry').

The fundamental SAM accounting principle is that sums for corresponding rows and columns should be equal – the matrix is a spreadsheet incorporating double entry bookkeeping from the national income and product (NIPA) and flows of funds (FOF) accounts maintained by many countries. The principles will be illustrated by tracing through row and column accounts as we go along.

The layout towards the top of the figure presents SSA's accounts on the left and ROW's on the right. Rows A through to E for each region summarise demand and production accounts. Rows E and F give private and government income flows, and rows G and H summarise their financial transactions or flows of funds. Import, export, and foreign aid flows appear in rows I through to M. The presence of so many trade rows underlines the complexity of Armington trade accounts.

To begin, row E states the sizes of the two economies. It shows that the sum of wage and profit incomes (or levels of value added or 'factor income') for the agricultural and industrial sectors in SSA are $60.55bn and $278.99bn in cells E-1 and E-2 respectively. The total, or 'GDP at factor cost' is $339.54bn in E-10. SSA's population is in the order of 725 million so that its GDP per capita is about $470 in these data. GDP in ROW is $29,482bn in E-19 (about 87 times as big as GDP in SSA). With a population of 5,725 billion, its GDP per capita is about $5,150. One region is far more affluent than the other (with by far the biggest share of ROW's GDP in the rich OECD countries).

Labour payments in SSA (not shown in the SAM) are 172.9, so that the labour share of GDP is 51.7 per cent. 'Profits' or all non-labour payments are 161.6. In the model presented below, total profits are set equal to profit rate x capital stock. If the SSA profit rate is 15 per cent, then the capital stock must be 161.6/0.15 = 1093.3 and the capital/output ratio is 1093.3/339.5 = 3.22 . These numbers are in the zone of plausibility. In ROW, on the other hand, the labour share is 56.3 per cent which is 'too low' by 15–20 per cent. At a profit rate of 10 per cent the capital/output ratio must be 4.37, which is 'too high'. As in other aspects described below, GTAP macro data for ROW should be regarded with scepticism.

The economic structures of the two regions differ in other ways. For example, agriculture accounts for 17.8 per cent of GDP in SSA, but only 6.9 per cent in ROW. Consumption levels of agricultural and industrial goods appear in cells B-3 and D-3 for SSA and B-23 and D-23 for ROW respectively. The shares of agriculture in the total are 34 per cent in SSA and 14.5 per cent in ROW, in line with 'Engel's Law' which asserts that the share of consumption devoted to food declines as per capita income rises. In two trading economies with such different income levels and structures, the assumptions underlying 'Utopian capitalism' necessarily come into question. It seems unlikely that the 'utility levels' underlying the two regions' respective little triangles are anywhere near being comparable.

Next we will look at cost of production and demand accounts.

Figure 3
Two country SAM: Sub-Saharan Africa and "Rest of the World"
1997 Billion U.S. Dollars. Source: GTAP Database 5.0, except Tariff data

SSA

		1	2	3	4	5	6	7	8	9	10
	SSA	Cost:A	Cost:I	Priv	Gov	Exp	Inv	M	Treas	Aid	SUM
A	M:A	35.82		6.64		14.31		-6.64			129.63
B	Armington:A	78.84	7.30					-6.64			
C	M:I		22.06				18.05	-40.10			
D	Armington:I	28.00	197.64	152.55	53.82	65.17	59.24	-40.10			517.51
E	Factor-Income	60.55	278.99								339.54
F	Gov-Income	-2.77	-6.82	41.34							42.20
G	FoF:Priv			66.81	-11.63		-59.24		-7.58	4.05	0.00
H	FoF:Gov								7.58		0.00
I	Imp(H,Agr)	2.41	0.71					6.64			9.76
J	Imp(H,Ind)	4.62	39.29					40.10			84.02
K	Exp(F,Agr)					-14.31					-14.31
L	Exp(F,Ind)					-65.17					-65.17
M	Aid									-4.05	-4.05
N	SUM	129.63	517.51	339.55	42.19	0.00	0.00	0.00	0.00	0.00	

	11	12	13	14	15	16	17	18
		10.25	Tariff Revenue				366.31	
		Incl Tariff	Incl Tariff Prices					Incl Tariff Incl Tariff
				Bilateral Trade Matrix				
				Intra-	Extra-	Extra-	Intra-	
				Regional	Regional	Regional	Regional	
				SSA	World	ROW	World	
				SSA	World	World	World	
				Prices	Prices	Prices	Prices	
		0.71	9.05	0.81	7.77	-7.77		
		7.49	75.78	67.66	-67.66	-530.84		
		8.24			13.70	-5,577.61	615.78	
		-0.61	-13.70	57.87	-57.87	530.84	15.62	
		-7.49	-57.87		4.05	5,577.61	58.25	5,856.49
		0.00					-4.05	0.00

ROW

		19	20	21	22	23	24	25	26	27	28		ROW
		SUM	Cost:A	Cost:I	Priv	Gov	Exp	Inv	M	Treas	Aid		
A		4,728.21	1,419.53	516.45	2,585.27		538.62		0.00			A	M:A
B			1,070.46	18,852.93	1,565.21			1,180.77	-331.65			B	Armington:A
C		48,771.86	2,042.70	27,439.85	15,196.00	4,291.94	5,645.27	6,461.23	-2,745.97			C	M:I
D		29,482.54	-117.50	-1,192.88					-2,745.97			D	Armington:I
E		3,545.36			4,489.42							E	Factor-Income
F		0.00			7,211.85	-746.58		-6,461.23				F	Gov-Income
G		-0.02								-750.62		G	FoF:Priv
H		-538.62					-538.62			750.62	-4.05	H	FoF:Gov
I		-5,645.27	206.88	92.87			-5,645.27		331.65			I	Imp(F,Agr)
J		631.40	106.13	3,062.64					2,745.97			J	Imp(F,Ind)
K		5,914.74										K	Exp(F,Agr)
L		5,856.49										L	Exp(F,Ind)
M		4.05									4.05	M	Aid
N			4,728.20	48,771.85	29,482.54	3,545.36	0.00	0.00	0.00	0.00	0.00	N	SUM

Macro-Balance SSA:

Private

Investment	Lending	Saving	G-exp.	Borrowing	G-Income	Export	Imports
59.24	7.58	66.81	53.62	-7.58	42.20	79.47	83.53

Ratio to Value Added: 339.54

S		I		G		Y-G		E		M		CA/GDP	Def/GDP
0.17		0.20		0.16		0.12		0.23		0.25		-0.01	0.03

Macro-Balance ROW:

Private

Investment	Lending	Saving	G-exp.	Borrowing	G-Income	Export	Imports
6,461.23	750.62	7,211.85	4,291.94	-750.62	3,545.36	6,183.88	6,179.83

Ratio to Value Added: 29,482.54

S		I		G		Y-G		E		M		CA/GDP
0.22		0.24		0.15		0.12		0.21		0.21		0.00

Column 1 shows that production cost in the SSA agricultural sector is made up of value added of 60.55 in cell E-1, plus intermediate inputs produced by the sector itself of 35.82 (cell B-1 – think of cattle feed grown on the farm, etc.), plus intermediates from industry (29.0 in D-1), plus imported intermediates comprising agricultural goods of 2.41 (I-1) and industrial goods of 4.62 (J-1). As discussed below, tariff payments are included in import valuations in cells I-1 and J-1. The remaining entry is -2.77 in cell F-1, which is a production subsidy paid by the government. The sum of all these entries is 129.63 in cell N-1, the 'gross value of output' in agriculture.

Row B summarises uses of agricultural products. Total supply is the 129.63 just mentioned plus a batch of 'final' imports (Gothic details below) of 6.64 for a total of 136.27. Of this, 35.82 goes for agricultural intermediate inputs as mentioned above, 7.3 for intermediate inputs into industry (B-2), 78.84 for private consumption (B-3), and 14.31 for exports (B-5). Row D for industry is similar, except that the sector also supplies capital goods for investment (59.24 in D-6).

Now we turn to foreign trade beginning with Row I for SSA, which summarises sources and uses of imports of agricultural goods. Including the price distortions due to tariffs they add up to 9.76 (US $bn) in cell I-10. The middle columns break down the sources. At 'world prices', 7.77 come from ROW (cell I-14) and SSA adds 1.28 in tariffs, to give a total of 9.76 in I-10. World price imports from within the region are 0.61 (I-13) to which 0.1 in tariffs is added to give a cost of 0.71 (I-11). Total supply at tariff-ridden prices in I-10 is 9.76 = 9.05 + 0.71.

Of that, intermediate inputs into agriculture take up 2.41 (I-1) and industrial use of imported agricultural intermediates is 0.71 (I-2). The remainder of 6.64 appears in I-7 as the 'final' imports mentioned above. To trace their destination we have to look again at rows A and B. The former simply says that final imports are 6.64 (the minus sign in A-7 is a trick to keep the SAM's internal accounting straight – more details below). And in row B, imports plus the gross value of production supply as discussed above.

We are almost at the stage of bringing in macro-economics. To get there, we first finish describing the external accounts in rows I-M of the figure, then turn to income-expenditure accounting, flows of funds, and finally macro balances.

We can continue tracing row I across the SAM. Recall that SSA's world price imports of agricultural goods from ROW are 7.77 in cell I-14. From ROW's point of view these foreign sales are exports, as represented by the sign flip between cells I-14 and I-15. Intra-regional ROW agricultural exports are -530.84 (I-16), giving total exports of -538.62 in I-19. This is the sum of the entries in row I for ROW. In fact, the row has only one entry (-538.26 in cell I-24). The sum of column 24 is zero, so the sign flips again in cell B-24, showing the export component of the agricultural sector demand–supply balance in ROW. Similar SAM accounting tricks (as proposed by Godley, 1996) are used in column 5 and row K to feed SSA agricultural exports of 14.31 into the ROW agricultural import balance.

There are two main income-expenditure balances for SSA, in row E/column 3 and row F/column 4. Private income is 339.54 in E-10. The same total appears in N-3, and column 3 describes its uses. There is consumption spending of 78.84 on agricultural goods (B-3), and 152.55 on industrial products (D-3). Direct taxes on the private sector are 41.34 (F-3) and it saves 66.81 (G-3). These four entries add up to 339.54. For ROW the direct tax is 4,489.4 (F-23) which is 15.2 per cent of GDP. This share is far 'too low'. The generous interpretation is that GTAP's number represents direct taxes net of the transfer payments that are a major component of fiscal spending in industrial economies.

SSA government income comes from the direct taxes in F-3 plus tariff receipts (10.26 in F-11) minus production subsidies paid to agriculture and industry (-2.77 in F-1 and -6.62 in F-2 respectively), for a total of 42.1 in N-4. Note that tariffs are about a quarter of government net income. One impact of liberalisation is to cut tariff receipts, which can be fiscally damaging in the absence of replacement revenues (which World Bank models blithely assume will be forthcoming from increased income taxes).

In most data sets the entries in F-1 and F-2 would be positive to take into account indirect taxes (VAT and so on) net of subsidies, but only the subsidy component is presented in the figure. Government uses its income to buy 53.82 of industrial goods (D-4). Like most governments around the world, it has negative saving of -11.63 in H-4.

Rows G and H give flows of funds. Standard FOF accounts distinguish between 'sources' and 'uses' for financial funds which must sum to zero for each 'institutional sector' (households, business, government, etc.). Sources are saving and increases in financial liabilities; uses are physical capital formation and acquisitions of financial assets.

The sign convention in the figure is that sources are entered positively and uses negatively. Thus in row G for the private sector its source of funds is saving of 66.81 (G-3). The uses are for investment (-59.24 in G-6; note the sign flip in bringing this number down from D-6) and new lending to the government (-7.58 in G-8). Because 7.58 + 59.24 = 66.82 the row sum is zero (apart from rounding errors). The numbers reflect the fact that private sectors very often save more than they invest, using the surplus to finance a fiscal deficit and/or an external surplus (as occurs for ROW in the figure).

The government has to cover its negative saving of -11.63 from other sources. These are the 7.58 it borrows from the private sector (H-8, again with a sign flip between rows G and H) and 4.05 in 'aid' from ROW. With appropriate changes of sign, the latter flow traces over to ROW in row M and column 29, where it becomes a use of funds for the ROW government in H-29.

Appendix 2

The Model in Algebra

1.1 Value Added

1.1.1 Price Level

$$w\sum_{i=1}^{3} L_i + r\sum_{i=1}^{3} K_i = \sum_{i=1}^{3} Q_i V_i \qquad (1)$$

$$\sum_{i=1}^{3} Q_i V_i = \sum_{i=1}^{3} \left(\alpha_i^{\theta_i} w^{1-\theta_i} + \beta_i^{\theta_i} r^{1-\theta_i}\right)^{\frac{1}{1-\theta_i}} V_i \qquad (2)$$

1.1.2 Distribution

$$\frac{wL_i}{(QV)_i} = \Omega_i = \left(\frac{\delta Q_i}{\delta w}\right)\frac{w}{Q_i} = \alpha_i^\theta Q_i^{\theta-1} w^{1-\theta} \qquad (3)$$

$$\frac{rK_i}{(QV)_i} = \Pi_i = \left(\frac{\delta Q_i}{\delta r}\right)\frac{r}{Q_i} = \beta_i^\theta Q_i^{\theta-1} r^{1-\theta} \qquad (4)$$

1.1.3 Factor Demand

Shephard's Lemma gives factor-value added ratios as

$$\frac{K_i}{V_i} = \left(\frac{\beta_i Q_i[w,r]}{r}\right)^{\theta_i} \qquad (5)$$

$$\frac{L_i}{V_i} = \left(\frac{\alpha_i Q_i[w,r]}{w}\right)^{\theta_i} \qquad (6)$$

Given the factor prices, these equations provide employment levels. Under the assumption of full-employment, exogenous total employment L^* would be constrained in

$$\sum_i L_i = L^* \qquad (7)$$

Under the full employment assumption, Shephard's Lemma determines the factor prices:

$$r = \left(\frac{K_i}{V_i}\right)^{-\frac{1}{\theta_i}} \beta_i Q_i[w,r]$$

$$w = \left(\frac{L_i}{V_i}\right)^{-\frac{1}{\theta_i}} \alpha_i Q_i[w,r]$$

so that the wage changes positively with V and Q.

1.2 Armington Prices

The domestic Armington prices are a CES-aggregate of the domestic price P, the market price of intraregional imports Z^{in} and the market price of imports from abroad, Z'.

$$Z_i = (a_i^{\sigma_i} P_i^{1-\sigma_i} + b_i^{\sigma_i} Z_i^{in\,1-\sigma_i} + c_i^{\sigma_i} Z_i^{\prime\,1-\sigma_i})^{\frac{1}{1-\sigma_i}} \text{ where} \tag{8}$$

$$Z_i' = \psi^{\prime xt} \tau_i^{xt} e Z_{fi} \text{ and } Z_i^{in} = \psi^{in} \tau_i^{in} Z_i \tag{9}$$

$\psi^{\prime xt} = (1 - z_E^{\prime xt})$ and $\psi^{in} = (1 - z_E^{in})$ are the price-reducing export subsidy factors on external and internal imports. Note that the market price of imports from abroad, Z', is increased by the domestic tariff rate on external imports τ^{xt} and decreased by the *foreign* subsidy rate $z_E^{\prime xt}$.

1.3 Domestic Price

$$P_i X_i = \sum_{j=1}^{3} h_{ji} Z_j X_i + \sum_{j=1}^{2} h'_{ji} \tau_j^{xt} \psi_j^{\prime xt} e Z_{fj} X_i - s_i X_i + Q_i V_i \tag{10}$$

$$P_i = \sum_{j=1}^{3} h_{ji} Z_j + \sum_{j=1}^{2} h'_{ji} \tau_j^{xt} \psi_j^{\prime xt} e Z_{fj} - s_i + Q_i \frac{V_i}{X_i} \tag{11}$$

$$\Rightarrow \mathbf{P}[\mathbf{Z}, \mathbf{w}, \mathbf{r}, \mathbf{e}] \tag{12}$$

We can write the linear unit cost function (the dual to the Leontief technology) as

$$P_i = f_i + (1 - f_i) Q_i \text{ where} \tag{13}$$

$$f_i \equiv \sum_{j=1}^{3} h_{ji} Z_j + \sum_{j=1}^{2} h'_{ji} \tau_j^{xt} \psi_j^{\prime xt} e Z_{fj} - s_i \tag{14}$$

f_i depends on input-output coefficients, tariff- and subsidy rates and varies with the latter two. The derivative of the cost function with respect to Q provides the usage ratio

$$\frac{\Delta P_i}{\Delta Q_i} \equiv \frac{V_i}{X_i} = 1 - f_i \tag{15}$$

1.4 Demand Functions: Domestic Product and Trade

Imports (and domestic product) are a function of composite supply and *final*, meaning tariff- and subsidy-ridden, prices. Shephard's Lemma provides the "real" levels of demand for domestic product and imports, given their relative prices.

$$X_i = \left(\frac{a_i Z_i}{P_i}\right)^{\sigma_i} A_i \tag{16}$$

$$M_i^{in} = \left(\frac{b_i Z_i}{Z_i^{in}}\right)^{\sigma_i} A_i \tag{17}$$

$$M_i^{xt} = \left(\frac{c_i Z_i}{Z_i'}\right)^{\sigma_i} A_i \tag{18}$$

Final nominal (Armington) imports of sector i goods, intermediate (Leontief) imports and total nominal imports are, in turn

$$M_{i,fin} = \left\{\tau_i^{in} Z_i \left(\frac{b_i Z_i}{Z_i^{in}}\right)^{\sigma_i} + \tau_i^{xt} e Z_{fi} \left(\frac{c_i Z_i}{Z_i'}\right)^{\sigma_i}\right\} A_i \tag{19}$$

$$M_{i,int} = \sum_{j=1}^{3} h_{ij}' \tau_i^{xt} e Z_{fi} X_j \tag{20}$$

$$M_i = \left\{\tau_i^{in} Z_i \left(\frac{b_i Z_i}{Z_i^{in}}\right)^{\sigma_i} + \tau_i^{xt} e Z_{fi} \left(\frac{c_i Z_i}{Z_i'}\right)^{\sigma_i} + \sum_{j=1}^{3} h_{ij}' \tau_i^{xt} e Z_{fi} \left(\frac{a_i Z_i}{P_i}\right)^{\sigma_i}\right\} A_i \tag{21}$$

1.5 Armington Material Balance

Total Armington composite supply is the sum of output across sectors:

$$\sum_{i=1}^{3} Z_i A_i = \sum_{i=1}^{3} P_i X_i + M_{i,fin} \tag{22}$$

$$\sum_{i=1}^{3} Z_i A_i = \sum_{i=1}^{3} \left[\sum_{j=1}^{3} h_{ij} Z_i X_j + Z_i C_i + Z_i G_i + Z_i Inv_i + Z_i Ex_i\right] \tag{23}$$

$$\sum_{i=1}^{3} P_i X_i = \sum_{i=1}^{3} \left[\sum_{j=1}^{3} h_{ji} Z_j X_i + \sum_{j=1}^{2} h_{ji}' \tau_j^{xt} e Z_{fj} X_i - s_i X_i + Q_i V_i\right] \tag{24}$$

where

- $Z_i C_i$ is the value of consumption of sector i Armington composite product,

- G_i – real government spending – is exogenous and equal to zero in the agricultural and industrial sector,

- Inv_i – real investment – is exogenous. $Inv_i = 0$ in the agricultural sector & services.

Using $X_i = \left(\frac{a_i Z_i}{P_i}\right)^{\sigma_i} A_i$ in the sectoral Armington material balance, we get the following expressions for real and nominal balances

$$Z_i A_i = \sum_{j=1}^{3} h_{ij} Z_i \left(\frac{a_i Z_i}{P_i}\right)^{\sigma_i} A_i + C_i + G_i + Inv_i + Z_i Ex_i \qquad (25)$$

$$A_i = \sum_{j=1}^{3} h_{ij} \left(\frac{a_i Z_i}{P_i}\right)^{\sigma_i} A_i + C_i + G_i + Inv_i + Ex_i \qquad (26)$$

Setting $D_{i,fin} = C_i + G_i + Inv_i + Ex_i$, letting a prime denote a column vector, bold face a matrix and a tilde a matrix with elements on the main diagonal the Leontief system is

$$A' = \mathbf{H}.\tilde{\boldsymbol{\chi}} A' + D'_{fin} \qquad (27)$$

$$A' = \left[\mathbf{I} - \mathbf{H}.\tilde{\boldsymbol{\chi}}\right]^{-1} D'_{fin} \qquad (28)$$

1.6 Macroeconomic Balance

$$\left[Z_2 Inv_2 - s[w,r] \sum_{i=1}^{3} \gamma_i X_i\right] + [Z_3 G_3 - Y_G] + \left[\sum_{i=1}^{2} Z_i Ex_i - \sum_{i=1}^{2} e Z_i M_i\right] = 0 \qquad (29)$$

1.7 Savings

The function for the sectoral savings rate $s[w,r]$ is

$$s_r \sum_i \Pi_i + s_w \sum_i \Omega_i \Leftrightarrow s_r \sum_i (1 - \Omega_i) + s_r \sum_i \Omega_i \Leftrightarrow s_r - (s_r - s_w) \sum_i \Omega_i \qquad (30)$$

$$s[w,r] = s_r - (s_r - s_w) \sum_i \alpha_i^\theta Q_i^{\theta-1} w^{1-\theta} \qquad (31)$$

$$\frac{\Delta s[w,r]}{\Delta w} < 0 \text{ with } \theta < 1 \qquad (32)$$

The level of savings for a given level of income then is

$$Sav = s[w,r] \sum_{i=1}^{3} Q_i V_i = s[w,r] \left(w \sum_{i=1}^{3} L_i + r \sum_{i=1}^{3} K_i\right) \qquad (33)$$

1.8 Consumption: Linear Expenditure System

Representative (indirect) utility maximization

$$\max \sum_i u_i[C_i] = \sum_i m_i Log(C_i - \xi_i) \text{ subject to } \sum_i Z_i C_i = D \qquad (34)$$

with $\sum_i Z_i \xi_i = F$ and $\sum_i m_i = 1$.

Derivation of the consumption function:

1. Frisch parameter: $\lambda = \frac{1}{D-F} \implies \frac{\partial \lambda}{\partial D} \frac{D}{\lambda} = -\frac{D}{D-F} = \beta \sim -2$

2. Engel elasticity: $\eta_i = \frac{\partial C_i}{\partial D} \frac{D}{C_i} = \frac{m_i D}{P_i C_i} = \frac{m_i}{\phi_i} \implies$ Engel aggregation $\sum_i m_i = \sum_i \eta_i \phi_i = 1$

3. Floor: $m_i(D-F)\frac{1}{P_i} + \xi_i = \frac{m_i D}{Z_i \eta_i} \implies \xi_i = \frac{D}{Z_i}(\phi_i - m_i \sigma^D)$ with $\sigma^D = -\frac{1}{\beta}$

4. Let $\mu_i = (\phi_i - m_i \sigma^D) = \phi_i(1 - \eta_i \sigma^D)$

$$C_i = (D-F)\frac{\eta_i \phi_i}{Z_i} + \xi_i \tag{35}$$

$$\sum_{i=1}^{3} \xi_i Z_i = F = D \sum_{i=1}^{3} \mu_i \tag{36}$$

$$C_i = D\left(1 - \sum_{i=1}^{3} \mu_i\right)\frac{\eta_i \phi_i}{Z_i} + \frac{D}{Z_i}\mu_i \tag{37}$$

$$= \frac{D}{Z_i}\left[\left(1 - \sum_{i=1}^{3} \mu_i\right)\eta_i \phi_i + \mu_i\right] \tag{38}$$

Total, nominal disposable income is the sum of sectoral value added less nominal savings and nominal (lump-sum) taxes.

$$D = (1 - s[w,r])\sum_{i=1}^{3} Q_i V_i - Tax = (1 - s[w,r])\left(w\sum_{i=1}^{3} L_i + r\sum_{i=1}^{3} K_i\right) - Tax \tag{39}$$

1.9 Welfare Function(s)

The representative utility maximization exercise in the Linear Expenditure System can be summarized as

$$u^* \equiv \sum_i u_i[Z_i, D] = \max u[C_i] \text{ subject to } \sum_i Z_i C_i = D^* \tag{40}$$

The dual problem to utility maximization is expenditure minimization:

$$D^* \equiv \sum_i e_i[Z_i, u_i] = \min \sum_i Z_i C_i \text{ subject to } \sum_i u_i[C_i] = u^* \tag{41}$$

The relation between the indirect utility function and the expenditure function is

$$e_i[Z_i, u^*] \equiv D^* \tag{42}$$

what means that the minimum expenditure at prices Z_i necessary to achieve the utility level u^* is income D^*.

1.9.1 Compensating Variation

$$\Delta D^{CV} = e[Z_i^{\mathbf{pl}}, u^{*,\mathbf{pl}}] - e[Z_i^{\mathbf{pl}}, u^{*,\mathbf{by}}] \tag{43}$$

1.9.2 Equivalent Variation

$$\Delta D^{EV} = e[Z_i^{\mathbf{by}}, u^{*,\mathbf{pl}}] - e[Z_i^{\mathbf{by}}, u^{*,\mathbf{by}}] \tag{44}$$

1.9.3 Functional Form

The original utility function and the consumption function from the optimization procedure are

$$\sum_i u_i[C_i] = \sum_i m_i Log(C_i - \xi_i) \equiv u \tag{45}$$

$$C_i = \frac{D}{Z_i}\left[\left(1 - \sum \mu_i\right)\eta_i\phi_i + \mu_i\right] \text{ and} \tag{46}$$

$$\xi_i = \frac{D}{Z_i}\mu_i \tag{47}$$

so that the level of utility as a function of prices and income is

$$u^* = \sum_i m_i Log\left[\frac{D}{Z_i}\left(1 - \sum \mu_i\right)\eta_i\phi_i\right] \tag{48}$$

The inverse of the (indirect) utility function gives the expenditure function

$$\exp^u = \exp^{\sum_i m_i Log\left[\frac{D}{Z_i}(1-\sum \mu_i)\eta_i\phi_i\right]} \tag{49}$$

$$\exp^u = \left[D\left(1 - \sum \mu_i\right)\right]^{\sum m_i} \prod \left(\frac{m_i}{Z_i}\right)^{m_i} \tag{50}$$

$$e[Z_i, u] = \left[\exp^u \prod \left(\frac{m_i}{Z_i}\right)^{-m_i}\right]^{\frac{1}{\sum m_i}} \left(1 - \sum \mu_i\right)^{-1} \equiv D \tag{51}$$

Evaluating the expenditure function at different utility levels and either base-year or post-liberalization prices gives the Equivalent and Compensating Variation, respectively.

1.10 Closure Rules

1.10.1 Elasticities: The Bank's Closure

- Exogenous: Government deficit, current account, (full) employment levels, current account

- Endogenous: Taxes, factor prices, exchange rate, investment

- **Public balance**: First, recall the government's balances. Exogenous variables are indicated by a bar. Budget constraint (with a fixed deficit), income and flows of funds are, respectively

$$Z_3\overline{G_3} + \overline{Sav_G} = Y_G^{Exp} \tag{52}$$

$$Sub + Tax + Sub_{Exp} + Tar = Y_G \Leftrightarrow Tax = Y_G - Sub - Sub_{Exp} - Tar \tag{53}$$

$$\overline{Sav_G} + B - \overline{CA} = 0 \tag{54}$$

$$Y_G^{Exp} = Y_G \tag{55}$$

The level of borrowing from the private sector B balances the flows of funds. The budget constraint – and therewith income – is fully determined from a given level of (negative) public savings and the exogenous level of real government spending, G_3. The value of Y_G still depends on Z_3, but nevertheless Y_G follows. With fixed subsidy- and tariff-rates, taxes adjust residually to match Y_G.

The government's accounts can be summarized as the difference between government expenditure, bonds and income, which has to equal the negative of the foreign deficit:

$$B - Sav_G = -\overline{CA} \tag{56}$$

- **Private balance**: With investment savings-driven, B determined in the government's flows of funds and savings a function of factor prices and value added, nominal investment is the difference between private savings and bonds, and real investment is

$$Z_2 Inv_2 + B - Sav = 0 \Rightarrow Inv_2 = \frac{Sav - B}{Z_2} \tag{57}$$

- **Foreign balance** The current account is fixed at the base-year level. e adjusts to revalue the trade flows such that this condition is satisfied.

- **Full employment constraint:** The full – or fixed – employment assumption, first, allows to endogenize factor prices and secondly, implies that shocks to the exogenous variables affect sectoral employment levels, but not the overall level of employment. Thus,

$$\overline{L} = L_{Agr} + L_{Ind} + L_{Ser} \tag{58}$$

$$\overline{K} = K_{Agr} + K_{Ind} + K_{Ser} \tag{59}$$

1.10.2 Absorption: A Keynesian Closure

Exogenous: Real investment, government spending on services, factor prices, exchange rate

Endogenous: Employment level (unconstrained), current account, government deficit

- **Private balance**: Savings are a function of wages and value added. With investment exogenous, B adjusts the private flows of funds:

$$Z_2 \overline{Inv_2} + B - Sav[w, QV] = 0 \Rightarrow B = Sav[w, QV] - Z_2 \overline{Inv_2} \qquad (60)$$

- **Public balance**: Revenue (Sub, Tax, Sub_{Exp}, Tar – in parts negative) determines government income, and the government adjusts its deficit in order to finance all expenditures. Thus, Sav_G is set in the first equation below. With B following from the private flows of funds, it has to be the current account that adjusts the government's flows of funds.

$$Z_3 \overline{G_3} + Sav_G = Y_G^{Exp} \qquad (61)$$

$$Sub + Tax + Sub_{Exp} + Tar = Y_G \qquad (62)$$

$$Sav_G + B - CA = 0 \qquad (63)$$

The balances are

$$B - Sav_G = -CA \qquad (64)$$

- **Foreign balance**: The CA adjusts to the fixed exchange rate.

- **Factor markets**: In this closure, employment is endogenous.

Acknowledgements

Edited by Emily Jones. Comments and editorial suggestions by Kevin Gallagher, Duncan Green, Emily Jones, Jamie Morrison, Sheila Page, Helen Shapiro, Catherine Barber and John Toye are gratefully acknowledged.

Endnotes

[1] Computable general equilibrium (CGE) modelling of trade liberalisation goes back more than 30 years. The first published paper known to the authors was by Taylor and Black (1974), who extended Leif Johansen's (1960) pioneering planning model to incorporate trade. The World Bank picked up on CGEs in general soon afterwards and has applied them ever since in many areas of its interest. With input from collaborators from Australia and Purdue with close connections to the Bank, the LINKAGE/GTAP specifications fit firmly within this tradition. Beyond the World Bank, many models of the effects of trade liberalisation have been constructed. There were two waves 15–20 years ago (with several contributions that were substantially more interesting analytically than the current crop) in connection with the Canada–US–Mexico debates about the CAFTA and NAFTA 'free trade' agreements. There have been numerous efforts subsequently in connection with the WTO negotiations. In the UK, HM Treasury (2004) lists more than 20 models that dealt with the Uruguay round, and at least as many address Doha.

[2] Most mainstream models choose elasticity values, which are high in comparison with econometric estimates.

[3] Figure 5 summarises the assumptions underlying the two closure rules.

[4] Ackermann (2005), Table 1, page 3.

[5] University of Chicago economics graduate students used to put out a calendar with caricatures of their professors. Harberger was the superhero 'Triangleman' with a diagram resembling Figure 2 emblazoned on his chest.

[6] ICTSD Bridges Weekly, 12 April 2006. See http://www.ictsd.org/weekly/index.htm (International Centre for Trade and Sustainable Development).

[7] In our two-region model, the origin and destination problem boils down to the question of whether imports are intra- or extra-regional: i.e. whether Namibia's imports come from, say, South Africa or from France.

[8] For historical reasons, imported and domestically sourced intermediates are assumed not to substitute for one another in response to price changes, an embellishment that can be traced back to Leontief's (1986) use of 'fixed coefficients' in his input-output tables.

[9] In some models some intermediate goods are imperfectly competitive.

[10] Just how these ideas get built formally into the analysis is taken up below.

[11] For the sake of simplicity, the economy discussed in the remainder of Part II concentrates on a *one-sector* economy, whereas our computer model has three. The principal findings from the former apply to the latter.

[12] For their own reasons, in their classic presentation of general equilibrium theory, Arrow and Hahn (1971) called it a 'Leontief economy' featuring cost-based pricing with constant returns to scale.

[13] We omit intermediate input flows. Intermediates both add to costs and contribute to demand; however, little insight is lost and a lot of notation saved if we leave them out of the discussion.

[14] For the moment it is convenient to value real output and demand flows at the price P. A slightly more general national supply price Z incorporating import costs is introduced below.

[15] The equation is $P(w,r) = (\alpha^\theta w^{1-\theta} + \beta^\theta r^{1-\theta})^{1/(1-\theta)}$ which mathematicians call a 'power mean'. That is, P is a fancy non-linear average of w and r with θ as the elasticity of substitution.

[16] Specifically, for a CES cost function the equations are $L/X = (\alpha/\omega)^\theta$ and $K/X = (\beta/\rho)^\theta$ so that the labour/capital ratio depends on input price ratios only: $L/K = [(\beta/\alpha)(\omega/\rho)]^{-\theta}$. Note how a higher value of θ implies that the input ratios respond more strongly to price changes.

[17] For better or worse, this 'consumption function' suppresses all analysis of how firms pass profit income to households via interest, dividends, and capital gains – World Bank models basically omit any financial transactions. They always set s_w equal to s_r even though data everywhere show that savings rates from profits exceed rates from wages.

18 This result follows from 'Walras's Law', which states that the price-weighted sum of excess demands (demand minus supply) for all markets in the economy must equal zero. No *single* market can fail to clear.

19 Along with a review of the underlying issues, the not overly felicitous 'closure' terminology was added to the CGE literature by Taylor and Lysy (1979). See also Taylor (2004).

20 Equations (P), (G), (M), and (F) as presented here are restated in somewhat more elaborate form below.

21 For the sake of simplicity, non-competitive intermediate imports are ignored in the following discussion.

22 In a closed-economy Keynesian model, the foreign trade term $(ZE - eZ^*E^*)$ should not appear in (M') and the two relevant flows of funds are (P') and (G') with the $e\Delta^*$ term omitted.

23 Rather than a lump-sum tax T, LINKAGE utilises an endogenous direct tax rate on household income, thereby adding a 'distortion' to the overall model.

24 There is not much new under the sun. In what is now called a 'Ricardo-Viner' specification, Taylor and Black (1974) sidestepped the problem of price over-determination by assuming that capital stocks are fixed by sector i so that each one has its own profit rate r_i driven via a cost function $P_i = P_i(w, r_i)$ by an output price $P_i = (1 + t_i)P_i^*$.

25 The distinction drawn in the Armington specifications between 'intra-regional' and 'extra-regional' imports is suppressed in the following discussion to keep the notation within bounds. We also omit a 'constant elasticity of transformation' embellishment (featuring a negative elasticity of substitution in a power mean) that separates domestic purchases and exports as sources of demand for total supply.

26 Again we use a CES specification, $Z = \{a^\sigma P^{1-\sigma} + b^\sigma [e(1+t)Z^*]^{1-\sigma}\}^{1/(1-\sigma)}$ which in a more complete formulation would include a term for costs of intra-regional imports as well.

27 That is, $X/A = (aZ/P)^\sigma$ and $E^*/A = [bZ/e(1+t)Z^*]^\sigma$ with σ as the elasticity of substitution between X and E^*.

28 An explicit formula for μ can be found by dividing the expression for X/A in footnote 23 into the one for E^*/A, and analogously for μ^*.

29 Dimaran et al. (2002) from GTAP quote Jomini et al. (1991) to the effect that their preferred '.... SALTER settings [of elasticity values] represent a compromise between econometric evidence and prior belief. A search of the econometric literature indicated that these elasticities are relatively low. Based on prior belief, it is generally still believed that the terms of trade effects of commercial policy changes are generally quite weak. Such weak terms of trade effects imply that the source substitution elasticities are relatively high. The SALTER settings adopted here thus represent a compromise: the elasticities are generally higher than those indicated by the econometric literature, but still low enough to generate significant terms of trade effects.'

30 Reducing export or production subsidies would have the opposite effect. Government net revenue would rise, meaning that direct taxes would fall to hold R constant. As it turns out, the LINKAGE closure with an endogenous lump-sum tax resembles Johansen's (1960) in his pioneering CGE simulations. But Johansen was using his model for medium-term sectoral growth projections and did not get distracted by the fiscal twists of tariff and subsidy changes (and certainly did not utilise the Armington apparatus).

31 For an explanation of the 'hat calculus' manipulations underlying the derivation of the equation in the text see Taylor 2004: pp54–6).

32 We used GTAP 5 because it was available in the public domain. Changes were made only to average applied tariff rates, based on recent World Bank publications that make use of the GTAP 6 data set. See World Bank Working Paper 3616, Anderson et. al. (2005), Table 1.

33 See the abstract in van der Mensbrugghe (2005).

34 The count according to Google seems to have risen since Charles de Gaulle's famous question, quoted in *Newsweek* in 1962: 'How can anyone govern a nation that has two hundred and forty-six different kinds of cheese?'

35 The features discussed are common to the overwhelming majority of global trade models.

36 LINKAGE papers usually refer to full (or fixed) employment in a footnote or abstract, but neither discuss it in detail nor attempt to justify the assumption.

37 Recall from previous discussion that 'closure' is CGE jargon for assigning causality in a model. The practice often boils down to deciding which variables should be exogenous or endogenous (or which equations should be included or excluded) to make sure the model is 'closed' or has a solution, like a typical problem from high school algebra.

38 We will see below how differently this assumption plays out in the 'rich' and 'poor' regions: in our 'developing country', either taxes jump up or government spending contracts dramatically in order to match the constraint on the deficit.

39 For a fairly comprehensive overviews of the Doha issues and negotiations, see http://www.ictsd.org/ or http://www.fao.org/trade/policy_en.asp.

40 We also examined different degrees of factor substitutability, but found little effect on the overall results.

41 Often, open-economy macroeconomics is undertaken under a 'small open economy' assumption, meaning that there are no repercussions of policy changes in the economy under study, on the rest of the world. As discussed in Part I, global CGE trade models apply to the whole world, and as we will see below there are effects on the large economy in other scenarios.

42 In contrast with the simplified model of Part II, the cost of output PX in any sector now incorporates the cost of intermediate inputs along with nominal value added $QV = wL + rK$ in which the 'price of value added' Q comes from a CES cost function of w and r.

43 Except for the outlier – agricultural imports from ROW to SSA – SSA exports increase by one per cent and other imports decrease by roughly one per cent, as the relative import price of agricultural product improves. Furthermore, the change in agricultural imports is approximately inversely proportional to the change in the tariff, which was 16.5 per cent on exports from ROW to SSA.

44 Due to the price decrease, the decrease in nominal terms is larger.

45 The following points suggest that if the economy is not artificially held at full employment, a CGE model is probably better suited to analyse the short-term rather than the long-term questions.

46 See Varian (1992). We report both Equivalent and Compensating Variation.

47 In this simulation, the external gap more than doubles, and the public deficit increases by 60 per cent.

48 As above, we discuss simulations with reasonable trade elasticities. Sensitivity analysis of simulations with Armington elasticities of the magnitude used in LINKAGE/ GTAP is presented below.

49 Eliminating only output subsidies increases welfare by more than 10 per cent and 5 per cent in SSA and ROW respectively.

50 The welfare measure shown in this graph is the average of Compensating and Equivalent Variation, relative to base year GDP. The former compares post- and pre-liberalisation expenditure (given the level of utility) at post-liberalisation prices; the latter does the same at base year prices. The measures are standard (see Varian 1992 and Appendix 2). Equivalent Variation tends to be lower and is therefore the more conservative measure; the World Bank usually reports this one. The difference between the two is small, on average.

51 Neither the USA's nor the EU's offers to reduce agricultural 'Amber' subsidies promise much more than domestic reforms and 'box-shifting' would have achieved in any case.

52 This clarifies the idea of the welfare measure: despite nominal decreases in consumption, welfare increases. Why? The welfare measure compares expenditure pre- and post-liberalisation as a function of 'real' utility out of consumption and prices. If the rise in the former outweighs the latter, welfare can increase despite a trough in nominal spending.

53 Kraev (2005) presents an analysis of the effects of trade liberalisation on GDP. Even though the model details differ, his methodology and aims are compatible with ours: endogenisng output, employment, and current account in a CGE framework allows us to estimate future risks or past losses due to trade liberalisation. The results presented by Kraev and those presented here are not

easily comparable. Government savings and foreign exchange inflows are fixed throughout scenarios, and either current account or employment (output) vary – which does not match either of our closure regimes. However, Kraev's research is consistent with the analyis presented here in the sense that, as soon as current account and employment are endogenised, trade liberalisation induces macroeconomic volatility – with mostly negative impacts on developing regions.

Oxfam International is a confederation of thirteen organizations working together in more than 100 countries to find lasting solutions to poverty and injustice: Oxfam America, Oxfam Australia, Oxfam-in-Belgium, Oxfam Canada, Oxfam France - Agir ici, Oxfam Germany, Oxfam Great Britain, Oxfam Hong Kong, Intermón Oxfam (Spain), Oxfam Ireland, Oxfam New Zealand, Oxfam Novib (Netherlands), and Oxfam Québec. Please call or write to any of the agencies for further information, or visit **www.oxfam.org**.

Oxfam America 226 Causeway Street, Floor 5, Boston, MA 02114-2206, USA Tel: +1.617.482.1211 E-mail: info@oxfamamerica.org www.oxfamamerica.org	**Oxfam Hong Kong** 17/fl., China United Centre, 28 Marble Road, North Point, Hong Kong Tel: +852.2520.2525 E-mail: info@oxfam.org.hk www.oxfam.org.hk
Oxfam Australia 156 George St., Fitzroy, Victoria 3065, Australia Tel: +61.3.9289.9444 E-mail: enquire@oxfam.org.au www.oxfam.org.au	**Intermón Oxfam (Spain)** Roger de Llúria 15, 08010, Barcelona, Spain Tel: +34.902.330.331 E-mail: info@intermonoxfam.org www.intermonoxfam.org
Oxfam-in-Belgium Rue des Quatre Vents 60, 1080 Brussels, Belgium Tel: +32.2.501.6700 E-mail: oxfamsol@oxfamsol.be www.oxfamsol.be	**Oxfam Ireland** Dublin Office, 9 Burgh Quay, Dublin 2, Ireland Tel: +353.1.672.7662 Belfast Office, 115 North St, Belfast BT1 1ND, UK Tel: +44.28.9023.0220 E-mail: communications@oxfam.ie www.oxfamireland.org
Oxfam Canada 250 City Centre Ave, Suite 400, Ottawa, Ontario, K1R 6K7, Canada Tel: +1.613.237.5236 E-mail: info@oxfam.ca www.oxfam.ca	**Oxfam New Zealand** PO Box 68357, Auckland 1032, New Zealand Tel: +64.9.355.6500 (Toll-free 0800 400 666) E-mail: oxfam@oxfam.org.nz www.oxfam.org.nz
Oxfam France - Agir ici 104 rue Oberkampf, 75011 Paris, France Tel: + 33 1 56 98 24 40. E-mail: info@oxfamfrance.org www.oxfamfrance.org	**Oxfam Novib (Netherlands)** Mauritskade 9, Postbus 30919, 2500 GX, The Hague, The Netherlands Tel: +31.70.342.1621 E-mail: info@oxfamnovib.nl www.oxfamnovib.nl
Oxfam Germany Greifswalder Str. 33a, 10405 Berlin, Germany Tel: +49.30.428.50621 E-mail: info@oxfam.de www.oxfam.de	**Oxfam Québec** 2330 rue Notre Dame Ouest, bureau 200, Montréal, Quebec, H3J 2Y2, Canada Tel: +1.514.937.1614 E-mail: info@oxfam.qc.ca www.oxfam.qc.ca
Oxfam GB Oxfam House, John Smith Drive, Cowley, Oxford, OX4 2JY, UK Tel: +44 (0)1865.473727 E-mail: enquiries@oxfam.org.uk www.oxfam.org.uk	

Oxfam International Secretariat: Suite 20, 266 Banbury Road, Oxford, OX2 7DL, UK
Tel: +44.(0)1865.339100. Email: information@oxfaminternational.org. Web site: www.oxfam.org

Oxfam International advocacy offices: E-mail: advocacy@oxfaminternational.org
Washington: 1112 16th St., NW, Ste. 600, Washington, DC 20036, USA Tel: +1.202.496.1170.
Brussels: 22 rue de Commerce, 1000 Brussels, Belgium Tel: +322.502.0391.
Geneva: 15 rue des Savoises, 1205 Geneva, Switzerland Tel: +41.22.321.2371.
New York: 355 Lexington Avenue, 3rd Floor, New York, NY 10017, USA Tel: +1.212.687.2091.

Linked Oxfam organizations. The following organizations are linked to Oxfam International:
Oxfam Japan Maruko bldg. 2F, 1-20-6, Higashi-Ueno, Taito-ku, Tokyo 110-0015, Japan
Tel: + 81.3.3834.1556. E-mail: info@oxfam.jp Web site: www.oxfam.jp
Oxfam India B55, First Floor, Shivalik, New Delhi, 1100-17, India
Tel: + 91.11.26693 763. E-mail: info@oxfamint.org.in Web site: www.oxfamint.org.in

Oxfam observer member. The following organization is currently an observer member of Oxfam International, working towards possible full affiliation:
Fundación Rostros y Voces (México) Alabama No. 105 (esquina con Missouri), Col. Nápoles, C.P. 03810 México, D.F.
Tel/Fax: + 52 55 687 3002. E-mail: communicacion@rostrosyvoces.org
Web site: www.rostrosyvoces.org